FARM GIRL

A MEMOIR

FARM GIRL

A MEMOIR

MEGAN BAXTER

GREEN WRITERS PRESS } *Brattleboro, Vermont*

Printed in the United States

10 9 8 7 6 5 4 3 2 1

Green Writers Press is a Vermont-based publisher whose mission
is to spread a message of hope and renewal through the words and
images we publish. Throughout we will adhere to our commitment to
preserving and protecting the natural resources of the earth. To that
end, a percentage of our proceeds will be donated to environmental
and social-activist groups. Green Writers Press gratefully acknowledges
support from individual donors, friends, and readers to help support
the environment and our publishing initiative.

Giving Voice to Writers & Artists Who Will Make the World a Better Place
Green Writers Press | Brattleboro, Vermont
www.greenwriterspress.com

ISBN: 978-1-9505845-4-3

COVER ILLUSTRATION: MIRABEL KERMOND

To Daniel

AUTHOR'S NOTE

This story is a work of nonfiction, which is to say that it is true, despite the storm of memory and the many seasons that separate what once was from what is now. Some names have been changed but everything else grows here as I remember it.

SEED

A seed contains all of a plant's potential, so when one is dropped into an open palm you hold a future of thick green leaves and the weight of summer-ripe fruit. In this way, all things begin to grow.

CHAPTER ONE

The cabin was everything that I'd hoped it would be. Remote, it pressed up against the dense forest of the Catskills and reflected by the mirror of a small pond in the front yard. It was like something out of Jayden's poetry—a dazzling little object, overwhelmed by beauty. As we parked in the gravel driveway and Jayden searched under the front porch for the hidden key, I could tell from the angry thrust of his arm that he didn't see anything charming about it. When I first saw the vacation home online, it reminded me of a place from our first summer together, isolated and heady with green. I'd been overcome with a rush of memory. Back then, when we were first in love, we would have laid out on the lawn stripped nude in the dappled sunlight, reading each other poetry and watching hawks spin like stars in the midday sky.

But those memories and those people seemed unfamiliar now. Jayden stabbed his hand blindly under the porch, fumbling for the key. "Fuck," he muttered, reaching deeper into the darkness, "God knows what's back here." His face was tight in a scowl as he spit out a list of potential dangers. I noticed that his body was shaking, vibrating really, like a bee in a flower. His curls hung damp and sticky against the back of his neck. Sweat pressed his T-shirt to his low back. His feet were dirty and bare as usual and something about the dig of his toes in the dark mulch turned my stomach. He'd grown up on the beaches of Malibu and always wondered why shoes were required anywhere. He put on a great show every time a grocery store rejected him, throwing his hands up in shock. Right up until the spring Jayden decided to become a poet and leave Los Angeles for an art school in Michigan, he'd been a successful child actor. In his last headshot, which I kept saved on my laptop, his eyes hold the camera with a sharpness that conveyed emotional authority and deep vulnerability. They were green and shot through with gold, like a cat's.

We'd driven the five hours to the cabin in relative silence, polite as strangers, waiting, I sensed, for the storm between us to build and break. I'd taken a few days off from Cedar Circle Farm, where I worked weeding, planting and harvesting vegetables and small fruit. It was my sixth summer at the farm and I'd begun to consider the place essential, like prayer. It felt, more than anything, like a chance to realize what was good in life. But Jayden and I needed to meet up somewhere that wasn't beloved, someplace which we could potentially share, savoring in memory like a slice of ripe melon. In planning our vacation I'd done everything I could think of to make it special. I'd bought us snacks and sodas, the same kinds which we'd passed between each other on so many road trips before. Together, with Dylan crying from the stereo and soda bottles sweating between our thighs, we'd driven the coast of California, the desert of Nevada, the high country of Oregon. We drove with the windows open, dark sunglasses beating back the sun, stopping for greasy hamburgers, cold beers, and cigarettes in the star-filled nights of the West. In those days we lived off candy bars and crackers and the gut-deep feeling that just over the horizon we'd find what we were looking for. We were hunters, united by love and a hungry emptiness which we never seemed able to satisfy.

Slipping into the mountains of Upstate New York, Jayden and I ate our snacks and sipped our drinks in silence. The salt and sugar burned my sun-chapped lips. An image of us together years ago slipped through my mind like a creature in tall grass, and I thought I would cry. An itchy heat would fill my throat and swallowing, I'd return to driving, my face set in a mask of composure. A confident girl. A happy girl. I'd made a mixtape for the drive, hoping, as I hoped for the cabin, that music would work some sort of magic on our love. I was always wishing for transformation, wanting to shed my skin and emerge changed, a butterfly, a garter snake.

After Jadyen and I first kissed, on a snowy beach in Michigan, he'd cried softly with joy and terror at the space blossoming between us. I felt him open to me like the pages of a book. At that moment we'd both transformed. He took me shopping on Rodeo Drive in his mother's Mercedes with the top down. I made handwoven editions of his poetry. We looked for signs everywhere in the world as if our lives were poems which we could read closely to understand: an orange full moon; cougar tracks in dew on the rocks of the San Ana Mountains; horses, all aligned head to tail, along the plains of Taos. Four years ago we would have talked long into the starry night about letters as if they were the only thing that mattered and imagined ourselves grown, constellations glittering in the dome of the sky.

But we had grown into creatures of different sorts. The air felt stormy in the car and each time either of us made a sound it seemed to strike a spark. Even the songs which had once been our favorites, the very soundtrack of our years, rang flat and overplayed. Dylan's voice whined and his harmonica buzzed like hornets trapped in a jar. Jayden flinched and turned the volume down. As my car rocketed over potholes on the back roads leading up through the mountains he braced himself in his seat, his knuckles white on the doorframe. In France, during eighteen holes of golf, he'd thrown his back out on a botched swing. He'd heard a sickening pop and doubled over in pain. The doctors said a disc had bulged out of line and it had been eating at him ever since.

"I hate the roads here," he hissed. "I hate the humidity. I hate..." he went on, listing the things that he hated, things that I loved. Trees, small towns, wildflowers. I let him list as I kept my hands tight on the wheel, hoping that he was just getting it out of his system, that it was the pain from his back injury talking.

At the cabin, after fumbling under the porch, Jayden shoved the key at me and wiped the dew from his fingers

onto his sweatpants. He stood and unfolded himself pain-
fully, his face dark and tight. I tried to smile but his eyes
were shining and flat, staring into some point beyond my
body. Night was coming to the yard, creeping in from
the forest. Pools of sunlight still lay hot on the grass and
rippled across the shimmering surface of the pond. I took
a deep breath, unlocked the door and carried our grocery
bags inside.

We paused at the threshold and my heart sank. The
curtains were lacy and crisp with age.

Mouse shit peppered the counters. Honey-colored lac-
quered pine boards glared with their knotted eyes from
the walls, ceiling, and floor. The place was like a bright
pine coffin.

"Why didn't we just get a hotel?" Jayden groaned and
flopped down across the dusty floral couch. He picked
up a remote and tried to get the TV working, clicking
through a blank screens. "Only DVDs?" He frowned and,
getting up again, scattered the stacked cases, searching
for something worth watching. I set the groceries on the
table and wiped the counters clean.

Then, I walked from room to room, taking stock of
the failure of the place. It was nothing like the pictures,
nothing like the memories I'd drawn up from that well of
hope. The turpentine smell of the pine boards was strange
and searing, like something preserved but ready to burst
into flames at the same time. In the ornate mirror above
the nightstand I looked into my eyes, heavy with exhaustion and brown. The girl who looked back was tired. I'd
curled my hair earlier in the day but the humidity had laid
it flat. Under my lids, my makeup was smudging and my

clothing, which I'd bought just for our reunion, felt too tight. I took everything off and stepped out of the puddle of fabric, the air cool on my skin. I walked into the living room naked.

"Put something on," Jayden said, scowling. "What are you doing?"

"It feels nice," I said. "I'm going to go outside and take a swim."

"Like that?"

"No one will see. We're all alone up here. Want to come?"

He shook his head and his green eyes were deeply sad. I wanted to go to him and hold his face in my hands but there was so much between us; the space between our bodies was country I couldn't understand or travel through. He was foreign to me. Instead of touching him I walked out, down the porch, through the wet grass of the yard and stood at the edge of the little pond. Sun lay on my shoulders like warm wings. I took one step into the mud, heard it slurp and open to my weight, then another, and sunk deep to my shins. The water was brown and warm. I looked behind me to see if Jayden was watching but the cabin's windows and doors were blank and flat as river stones. What was I doing, I wondered, standing naked at the edge of the water? The pond's surface flattened and became a mirror again, reflecting the sky and my body's warped shadow. Even without the press of my new clothing, I didn't feel like myself. I'd been so many girls for Jayden but now I didn't know if he wanted any of them. How could I transform this time?

I remembered swimming in freezing mountain water years ago on one of our drives along the long spine of California. The river ran white through the current's heart, clear at the edges. Jayden lit a cigarette as he watched me from the roadside. His long body leaned on the car's hood, sizzling hot at high noon. In a white dress, I was my own vision of a teenage dream, on a desert road, in a fast car. I took off my boots and stepped onto the smooth bank, one foot and then another until I sunk to my knees. The cups of my bra filled, spilled out snow-melt. All day— in the desert, in the car—the smell of that ceremony followed us, as fresh and old as the river itself. Jayden had said I tasted like water and I imagined myself altered by the current's touch.

At the pond's edge, I spun the gold wedding band on my finger until the metal grew warm from my grip. All those days and years were fused into that ring. I remembered the night we'd slipped them onto each other's fingers, how we'd watched fireflies flickering in the dusk and promised *forever*. I'd bought the bands with money from a poetry prize and somehow, because of this, they felt forged from words. Words had brought us together and ran, like bedrock, beneath our love. But we'd hardly written a thing in four years, despite our constant striving to put pen to paper. Instead, we devoured other people's words as if reading would save us. We collected books and made fortresses out of their dusty spines. But the pages of our journals lay like blank faces. The words that had once rushed through our heads like mountain streams had run dry.

With cupped hands, I reached down and scooped water up to my face. I let it run down my skin from chin to navel, all the way along my thighs until it joined with other water. It smelled organic, like the forest floor at dusk, the loam darkly breathing, and made me feel like I was bathing in soil, in the rich brown earth. At the edge of the treeline, a fawn and her mother stepped into the last light, as silent as dreams. Their ears rotated towards me and they froze.

I didn't move. They came to me slowly, drawn to the water. I held my breath. Across from me, the little one lapped at the pond creating ripples that spread against my ankles. She was so close I could count her spots. Then, suddenly, a noise from the cabin, a crash, and they bolted into the darkness of the underbrush, jumping through blackberry and jewelweed. I let out a deep breath and turned to face the cabin. All summer this night had been brewing. I couldn't avoid it any longer.

At the farm, June hits like a storm. I am there seven days a week and when work ends at four in the afternoon, I sit long into the evening by the riverbank sipping cool beers with Nick and Luke, growing stories like veins. My legs are strong from biking. My arms and back are deep tan. When I jump off the dock soil runs off my skin and back into the river whose ancient flooding created the alluvial fields I plant, harvest, and sweat in. My body is never just mine; there are always traces of river and dirt, salt and the thin green sap of growing things.

At home, my mother scolds me if I walk into the house wearing my worn work boots. She makes me scrub the dirt out from under my nails before dinner. She has me leave my pants at the door.

"Your skin," she says as my first sunburn flakes off, revealing a deep tan glow.

"Your nails," she says as she sees me cut them low, scooping out soil from beneath their white crescents. To win her favor I bring her bags of vegetables and fistfuls of flowers, and gift by gift she warms to the idea of her oldest daughter as a farm girl.

But I have no time to think of nails and boots and gifts in June. Suddenly the white strawberry flowers become green berries. It happens in the long steady light of the solstice. The little fruit turn from green to white and in a week of heat they flush from a light pink into a deep red. Before I can imagine the fruit, hanging like jewels under the dense green leaves, it is strawberry season.

I wake early. All night I walk through dreams of the farm—I plant and harvest and weed in my sleep. I stir every hour through the darkness to look at the red numbers on the clock, counting down my time of rest. Three more hours, two more hours, half an hour until the faintest light breaks at the edge of the world and my body is called up from the sheets.

June is the hardest month and the most vital. It can't be ignored. June sits in the very middle of the year when the days are longest and fullest. It is somehow both the start and the heart of the season. Most everything has to be planted in the first weeks of the month while the earliest crops are ready to harvest already. Strawberries are ripe by the end of the month and the farm is flooded with people picking them. The berries are the farm's highest-grossing crop and their management, which is my job, drives my exhaustion. Most years I have one day off in June, the day after our annual Strawberry Festival. I sleep in, my hands stained red from the fruit, my knees pocked with straw dust.

The berries need to be picked fresh every morning and the strawberry shack, where customers check in before heading to the fields, needs to be staffed, boxes folded, quarts ready to hand out, the scale charged, the road signs changed from open to closed. The big irrigation pipes need to be moved through the patch on the warmest days and hooked up to the pump so their sprinklers can cool ripe fruit. At the same time, the rest of the farm needs to be planted; rows of tomatoes, peppers, eggplants, melons, lettuce, corn, and squash have to be laid in by whoever isn't working in the berry fields. And in the mornings the crew also has to harvest the first vegetable crops, wash them, pack them in crates and deliver them for sale.

Every June morning begins with a survey of the strawberry fields and I walk to them religiously, like a monk to prayer. I am drawn to the fields—my feet know the path down from the barn and I am pulled out magnetically. I don't think I can be swayed even if I'd wanted to. *Good morning*, I say, quietly, walking with my hands palm down over the rows as if I can feel them rising to me. My course through the patch is a zigzag survey of each variety, deliberately random. Sometimes the front or back of a row can ripen at different times due to the slow shift of shade from the hedgerow so I have to cover all four fruiting acres, back to front, side to side. The dew is heavy and my shoes and lower legs are soaked by the time I finish. Every few paces I stop and sink to my knees and lift a cluster of berries in my palm. I twist it side-to-side, checking for ripeness, firmness, and color. When I am down in the straw the field envelopes me and I vanish into the plants and fog.

Through this daily sampling, I develop a sensitive palate. Every morning I eat a few to register sugar levels on my tongue. A tart berry has a few days on the plant, An almost boozy, overripe fruit has to be picked as soon as possible. I read the weather report online every hour so I can look forward and forecast heat and rain and how the fruit will respond. Does it need water to grow fat or sun to ripen hard berries? Does the patch need a day or two of cooler weather to slow down a quickly ripening field, or does it need heat to raise sugar content? I weigh these things in my hands with the berries.

In the patch, I decipher how many quarts lay ripe in the field ready for picking, and how long the picking that will last. The best fruit we harvest ourselves to sell at the farm stand and markets. These are usually the king berries, the first fruit set by the plant. My staff of pickers works ahead of people who come later and harvest for themselves. I stick different colored plastic flags at the start of each row to indicate who picks there first. One color for pick-your-own, one for my crew. They flutter brightly. Walking out of the fields, wet, my fingertips stained red,

I fill out numbers on a pick sheet in the strawberry shack where the air is always cool and dusty. I write my notes in a journal, *Jewels great today, still picking Mesabi, will be open until Friday.* The pages are curled and damp from the dew's humidity. By the end of the summer the book will appear ancient, like some record from another time.

What I really learn to read on those mornings, and what I can't even describe, is a feeling. It is potential energy—a hovering, wave-like thing that rests right about the plants in the field like low fog. To read it I have to sink to my knees. I sink further. I sit in the damp straw aisles and raise my hands, palms down over the leaves and spread my fingers. A patch full of ripe fruit feels warm and pulses against my hands. A patch full of fruit about to ripen shimmers with possibility.

I call it my *spidey senses* like Spider-Man develops after his bite, on the verge of human and insect. I quote Han Solo too: *I have a bad feeling about this*, a gut reaction that is part experience, part fortune-telling. I learn to read the fields with this strange sense throughout the season, even when there are no more berries to harvest. In August when the plants are big and full, in November when they crumple into red foliage—but they never feel as alive, as radiant, as they do at dawn in June.

While I am out in the fields the rest of the farm crew starts to trickle in. Their cars drift quietly through the fog, headlights illuminating the parking lot and rolling out over the banks of vegetation casting rotating shadows in the straight rows. Luke, the field manager, turns on music in the processing area under the tin roof of the barn and the beat rattles the beams. I can hear it echo off the pine trees across the river. The whiteboard in the washing area becomes a harvest list. I am always picking or managing strawberry pickers so I can only see the crew arrive from a distance. They gather around the board, count out rubber bands, grab knives or scissors and load harvesting totes into the back of the truck. Their bent-over bodies move slowly through the fields across the road from the berries. Occasionally, a crew member takes the truck back up to the barn, the bed loaded with greens.

Luke fills big metal sinks with cold water and washes the produce as it comes in, carefully completing the order forms from restaurants, stores, and the farm stand. He works fast, moving bunches from sink to sink and into black crates or wax boxes. The drumline of his music drifts down into the fields. Nick, the equipment manager, starts up Yoda, the farm truck, a red Toyota pickup with white dashes on the side, California license plates, and a friendly, square face, which we call Yoda. Yoda has no model name, just the year 1990, to mark its birth. It is barn red with a black plastic bed liner. Its old engine whines as it cycles. I walk up as if drawn to the noise and, waving good morning, slip into the farmhouse to make photocopies of my notes. I leave copies of them like horoscopes on the desk by the phone and on the farm stand counter near the register so that our retail staff can know what I know in the fields at dawn. By our "pick-your-own" entrance, I switch out the CLOSED sign for the OPEN sign, slipping the hooks through the eyes. Words sway in the fog along the roadside. With the patch open and my notes shared, I walk back down to the strawberry patch to meet the pickers.

Bill, the man who trained me, retired years ago, and I've become the strawberry crew leader. I hold up fruit for kids just like Bill once held them up for me and I tell them which berries are good and which are bad. I collect the picked quarts they leave behind in the rows and tally their numbers at the end of the morning.

When bad bunches of beets or rotten lettuce come up to the barn, I can hear Luke cursing and tossing plastic totes around. "What the fuck is this shit?" He turns up the music and works faster, yelling over it to the crew as they finish the harvest. When picking is complete the crew hitches a truck up to the flatbed trailer lined with trans-plants. A few people drop the starts out of the tray onto the row and everyone else follows behind planting. Then they move pipes and set up irrigation and Nick turns on the old tractor by the river. The Rain Bird sprinklers sput-ter then burst and cast long arches of river water over the newly planted rows.

By lunch, everyone has said every mean thing they could think of to each other. We call each other mother-fuckers, bitches, assholes, hippies, princesses, and idiots. We all talk about quitting, starting our own farms, and doing everything our way. But as the heat increases, we settle.

In June we eat lunch by the river and Luke will often give us a full hour instead of the usual half so that the crew can swim and relax. We sit around on the steps of the cabin smoking cigarettes. A few guys slip off to suck on pot pipes behind the tree line. We take turns diving when the river is high, yelling out points like judges at the Olympics. When the river is low, we cannonball off the dock, exploding into the brown water. By the end of the month, only the current in the very center of the river is cold.

In the afternoons I go back to the strawberry fields while the rest of the crew weeds or keeps planting. Some days Luke surprises us at quitting time with popsicles or ice cream, or better yet, cold Coronas and a bag of limes. The crew piles into the back of a pickup truck and speeds down to the river, the tires kicking up silt. There we smoke in the shade, dangle our legs off the dock, lodge limes in the throats of cold beers, lick cherry popsicles or lie in the grass looking at the big clouds roll away.

June is the month that forms friendships and alliances. There isn't any other way to get through. The crew bickers and comes together again day after day until we build a mythology forged out of hard work. We repeat stories about disasters averted, the coldest mornings or the hottest afternoons until we've written sagas. In this way, we become the heroes of our own legends.

They are little things mostly, tiny stories that only matter at the farm between the people who were there to see it and tell it. The afternoon when all the gears except reverse failed on a tractor and Luke drove it from Alice's, one mile away, backward, looking over his shoulder. The day Luke and I planted strawberries while being swarmed by angry bees. There are stories of successes too, the market when Robert and I sold $2,000 in strawberries and came back to the farm with a stuffed cash box. We show-ered twenty-dollar bills over Nick and Luke who were drinking at a picnic table in the shade and repeated the M.I.A. lyrics which had become something of an anthem.

In June the year is made or lost so money is always on my mind. Bad weather can ruin the berry crop or bog down the tractors, preventing the fields from being planted, setting back the rest of the season. A crew might fail to come together and splinter and need mending for the next four months. Everything is magnified by that stress so joy in June is bigger than it is any other month; success means more. Busy days and good harvests fill me with incredible pride.

Overwork and sleep deprivation reduce my world to the point of simplicity. Food tastes better, beer is colder, water on my skin is like a baptism, clearing away a day of toil and sweat.

CHAPTER TWO

Jayden was pouring tequila into a glass of ice when I walked back into the cabin, painted to the knees with socks of muck.

"I'll make you one after you shower," he said. He took a long drink and his cheeks filled with the flush that I remembered from our years in cold winters. From Michigan to Maine I'd loved his chilled face, our walks in the snow, our hands stuffed into each other's pockets. Was there a road atlas back to that time? I wondered, under the shower's hot stream. Little by little, we'd slipped apart and then over the course of a summer something huge had grown between us. Maybe it had been there all along, too deep a cut to shift, no matter how hard I tried to shimmy my way into the form of a girl he'd love. I'd bought designer jeans, had my hair cut by celebrity stylists, and learned to use every utensil set out at a five-course tasting menu. All this, I had done for him. To get closer. To leave behind my small town New

England manners, *please* and *thank you* and a straight back always. Being Jayden's was my greatest shape shifting act.

I imagined the lips of the Grand Canyon which we'd walked together, the shelves of Zion, the pillars of Bryce, rock monoliths separated by time. Back then, when we'd hiked and posed for pictures in those brilliant Western sunsets, we had seemed like two halves of one person. Cut from the same material. But now, seeing him toss tequila down his throat, I felt something hard and heavy sink in me. I rubbed my skin dry with the towel and wrapped it up tight.

As Jayden poured me a drink in the kitchen, I rummaged through our bags for a T-shirt and jeans. Throwing one of his sweatshirts aside a condom, still wrapped and crisp, fell out of the pockets.

I held the foil pinched between two fingers as if it could burn me. He hadn't gotten this for us. After all, I'd been on the pill for years. I turned the wrapper side to side as if it was some kind of joke, a fake, anything but itself. I walked with it out in front of me, carrying it like a woman might carry a lantern into a dark space. It electrified the air between us. My fingers tingled, crackled the foil, started to sweat and stick. My arms began to shake holding up its tremendous weight. All I could do was cling to it, even as it began to quiver, even as my muscles started to fail.

"What the fuck is this?" I demanded, holding it out, damning him. His eyes found it before they found me. The green and gold of them narrowed in on the shining foil and I watched as his features were erased, like the sky after a great storm. All the clouds of bitterness swept away.

"I didn't use it," he said. There was a sharpness to his voice that said *fight* but I could tell he knew there was no way out, no fit or scene that would make it go away. He dropped his head, tumbling his curls over his eyes. As all the anger left him his shoulders softened. "I'm sorry," he said. "It was just in case."

I felt tears on my cheeks before my chest started to crumble into sobs. I fell to my knees on the shining pine floors and tossed the thing out away from me. I wanted only to hold myself and feel that wholeness surrounding my heart, binding it. He'd dreamed of, thought of, even planned to sleep with another girl. Something in the deliberate intent of that purchase, how he opened a box somewhere in Paris and tore one from a sheet of possibilities and slipped it into his pocket, knowing, probably hoping, he might need it later on some night when I was heavy with sleep, my dirty legs and feet staining my sheets, dreaming of strawberries and silt. He'd reached out, but not to me. Just like that he'd rejected any future we might share. Erased it. Cut me out like I was in the past tense.

Jayden knelt beside me and put his hands on my shoulder. "I'm sorry," he said softly. "I didn't know what we were."

"We were engaged!" I said through a river of tears.

"I guess," he whispered. "Just this summer . . . I don't know who you are anymore."

My face turned hot and my tears began to dry up in salty rivers. I felt myself quaking, as if something deep under my skin, some huge creature, was stirring. I erupted, pushing him off before my hands became fists or claws that wanted only to dig and strike at him. I backed myself away into a corner, putting empty air between us.

"I've been writing," he said, firmly, crossing his arms as if the statement settled our argument. There and then, easy as that. He looked so smug, I thought, so confident. He said softly, "Isn't that what we're supposed to be doing?" I absorbed his barb but it stung me, and for a moment I forgot the rip, the tear in my chest where my heart was heavy and beating at my broken ribs. If not love then words. If not words then love. Slowly I came out of my corner. My arms were heavy and hung at my side. He uncrossed his and set them on the counter, reaching for the liquor bottle. I had trapped us in the cabin. There was nowhere to go. We could only stay and try to make it right.

The loneliness, the isolation of that night watched us from outside the windows like a monster. We made spaghetti. We poured tall glasses of tequila. Tears became dry and then they became howls and the howls became whispers full of spit and I stopped being able to see straight for a while. We dug things up and then buried them. It was methodical, this undoing.

At some point in the night, Jayden went outside to smoke a cigarette and didn't come back in. After a long stretch of silence, when the sounds of the forest seemed to rise and rage, I stood and waded through the tequila. He was sitting on the porch steps, his back hunched. He could have been an old man, not the boy I'd fallen in love with in high school. There were filters crumbled around him and he was sucking orange sparks out of another.

"Jayden," I said.

"I just want to be alone," he whispered without turning to me.

My eyes tried to make tears but they'd gone dry hours ago. I lay back on the couch, poured the rest of the tequila into my glass, and slipped a DVD into the TV. It was a plastic surgery reality show, hours of it, and I watched as people were transformed, pulled apart, emptied, and re-stitched. Did they wake up feeling better? Did they look in the mirror and finally know themselves? I wondered. I fell asleep as yellow fat was weighed and dark sutures were drawn through the eye of an open wound.

A cornfield at dawn is how I imagine the beginning of the world in the Garden of Eden. Every surface drips with water. The sky and the earth meet as the fog hangs low so walking through the field you are also in the clouds, mist clinging to the little hairs on your arms and earlobes. Sweet corn grows about seven feet tall. Each row becomes its own labyrinth, cutting you off from everything except leaf and stalk and mist. In the cornfields a person can get lost, directions fade, the start of the row looks like the end and the middle is one long stretch of tassels. The world is reduced to rows of wet stalks. Mornings are dark and heavy with fog. Water is everywhere, in the grass, on the plants, condensed on the truck's windshield, dripping from the slick leaves of the oak trees by the river's edge.

Maps, even mental maps, shrink as the fog confines visibility to a few hundred feet. Houses, cars, fishing boats on the river appear and then vanish like ghosts. The mist absorbs sound so there is no noise except the chanting of birds and bugs, pulsing inhuman rhythms from the edges of perception.

We pick sweet corn fresh every morning. The sugar in its kernels begins converting to starch as soon as it's snapped off the stalk. Fresh sweet corn, husked in the field, is so sweet sugar sticks to your cheeks and hands. Corn is heavy, a full bushel basket weighs about forty-five pounds. So that wet, and sticky, and burdened, I push through the tight rows, lost in the fog.

Unlike tomatoes or strawberries, which signal ripeness through color, corn is wrapped up and hidden. A farmer has to look for more subtle signs, which might change variety to variety or even season to season. Ripe corn appears full, pressed against the husk. The tassels have dried down to a matted dark brown and if you pinch the top of the ear, the very tip of it, it should feel juicy. The kernels ripen from the bottom up and only when an ear is fully ripe will the kernels at the tip have filled out with sugar and water. Just to be sure I pick a few ears, strip them quickly and bite into them, sucking the sweetness between my teeth and tossing the cob to the birds.

Robert, a boy my age with broad square hands and a trucker hat, picks corn with me every morning except for Sunday—our one day off—and Saturday, when we pack up early for the farmers market. The corn grows at Alice's, a rented property a mile down the road. We harvest into sling bags that loop over our shoulders and hang near the hip. Each bag can hold a bushel. They are sold mostly to apple orchards, but at the farm, they make handy containers for corn, artichokes, and peppers. As they fill, they grow heavy and pull me down to one side. To empty the bags, I hold them over a bushel basket, unsnap two rings and open the cloth bottom. Lightened, standing suddenly straight, I slip back into the rows.

Robert and I lose each other in the field. Each of us takes one row and walks it until we reach the point where we stopped the previous day. The stems of the corn we already picked are browned and hang loosely from the stalk, broken from our trespass. Harvesting corn requires tracking, reading the plants, reading the rows, following the prints of animals and the flight of birds. Raccoons pick corn off the plant carefully. They strip the ears on the ground and eat bare to the cob. Crows pull at the husks from the top, scratching and pecking into the kernels, leaving the ears scarred and exposed but still attached to the plants. Bears tear up whole sections of the rows, like small storms—dragging stalks, crashing through weeds, trailing broken plants behind them. Our bootprints mix with the animal tracks. We follow ourselves deep into the field.

Sometimes I can hear Robert snapping off the ears or the brushing of corn leaves as he turns and heads out to the truck. Other times the fog blankets all noise and I am alone. I listen, waiting for the birds and bugs to mean something, to rise to something beyond their drone. Then I fall into a steady pace, ripping corn off the stalk and slipping it into my bushel bag.

I am wet as soon as I step into the rows. The plants and the weeds reach over my head and each time I touch them dew scatters down, seeping into my socks and soaking my boots, dripping down my arms, down the back of my neck, through the waistband of my shorts. The bag grows heavy with corn and water and presses into my thigh. I walk like I'm crippled; stiff-legged, hauling the ears out to the road. From the truck I try to find Robert in the field, looking for shaking corn stalks or the flash of his light-colored hat.

Picking corn stays with me all day. My clothing barely dries, despite the heat, and sharp leaves lash my arms and legs. Bug bites swell in the hidden folds of my knees and neck and I lean slightly to the side as if the weight of the bag still pulls me over. The rhythm of corn picking is dreamlike, snap, slip, snap, slip, walking through a world that as soon as the sun burns through the fog is clearly defined as rows, fields, acres, river, road, hills.

But in the morning, the universe is still small and mystical. Anything can appear in the mist. Once, as I finish picking and slam the tailgate shut, the clouds lift and I can see a bald eagle, gliding over the river. He spins and spins and then comes in close to the water, talons dropping and with a hard splash rises again, a fish thrashing in his grip. The great birds nest along the river, in a grove of tall white pines. They are indicators, the town paper says, of the returning health of the riverway, just like our tall green corn stalks are signs of the soil's vitality.

In these moments I look at myself from a distance, leaning on the red body of an old Toyota truck, my face sticky with a breakfast of fresh sweet corn and think, *how lucky, how odd, how beautiful.* I imagine people waking up with their shades closed or driving through the fog and seeing nothing of these things. I feel privy to the world's secret moments, to the time when mornings become afternoons, nights fade to days, to the goings-on of bears and birds, the smell of low clouds, the subtle shift, on that first cold morning, from summer to fall. This knowledge fills me like words and I know that I am where I am meant to be. The world is small and I am just an animal in it, like the bears and raccoons, hunting for sugar in the wet rows.

CHAPTER THREE

Morning light hit me and crawled up my body, toe to shoulder until it was laying on my eyelids. I pulled myself up into the wave of a hangover, my head filling with blood, my mouth dry as gravel. My eyelashes were cakey with tears and my lips tasted like salt. I could feel my heartbeat pounding around in my skull. Our clothing was scattered everywhere. At some point early in the night, we'd tried to make love, hoping that might fix us, but it had only made us more aware that there was nothing lovely between our bodies. Just history and something like respect turning to bitterness in the cask of time. I'd reached for the boy I'd loved four years ago on a Michigan campus, a boy with wild curls and a dark peacoat and pockets full of poems and found instead a young man, electric with booze, muddled and messy and miles away from me. Jayden had reached for the girl he'd kissed on a snowy beach, a girl with a long dark coat and pockets full of poems and touched a strange, tanned farmer, this girl with dirt still in the creases of her knees, her hands so calloused they brushed him roughly. We hadn't been able to connect our ghosts. We'd only made our different forms more apparent.

Jayden was in the bedroom, asleep on top of the covers. His long body was wrapped around a lacy pillow and his face was soft. I stopped and looked at him, trying to make myself remember him beautiful. His lips were slightly open and under the thin skin of the lids, his eyes drifted in dreams. He was so peaceful that I felt ashamed for yelling like I had the night before. But even the memory of yelling throbbed my hungover head. I scooped up his clothing and lay it near him. Under the shower, I scrubbed until I was pink and then brushed my teeth with hot water so inside and out, I felt clean. As soon as I left the bathroom and went to watch the morning from the porch, I realized that I'd rather be anywhere but where I was. We were in twilight, a grey area between love and separation, where everything needed to be deliberately navigated and named.

I knew we were far from over. Across the country, in Portland, Oregon, we still paid rent on an apartment. The lease was in both our names. We shared a cat, living for the summer with my parents, and a college. There was no way to run from Jayden. We couldn't simply split. And still I wondered, feeling my teeth get hairy again, my breath dry, if maybe we could make it work. Or at least be friends. After all, we'd practically grown up together. But we'd also grown apart, grown separate. Who was I if I wasn't Jayden's?

I rested my heavy head in my hands as the early August cicadas started to whine from the wood line. Still, we had the whole day together, a long drive home, three meals, and a shared bed. Still, we had to keep reaching for each other like we knew who the other was. Inside I heard Jayden stepping onto the pine floors, groaning. My heart sank. Why was I here when I could be back at the farm? Why had I wasted this morning with Jayden, with a tequila hangover, when I could be picking corn?

Our break started when Jayden left for Paris that summer. I hadn't been able to go with him, despite his many invitations. I stayed at the farm because I needed money, something Jayden struggled to understand. Working seven days a week for two months if the weather allowed helped me pay off my car loan, buy groceries and cover rent during the school year.

Jayden's parents paid for everything and his occasional royalty checks from his mild success as a child actor made him feel richer than he really was; he'd buy art prints, or a new wardrobe when those checks appeared, unexpected in the mail after a re-run played or some DVDs were sold in China. Jayden believed that he needed Paris to help his poetry, which had slowed to a mid-summer stream, drained by depression. He felt that I needed it too. "I was," he said, "becoming something of a hick."

You're only half alive unless you're writing, he messaged me. *How is my country bumpkin?* he'd write later. *I think of you on your acres by the river. I wish you were in the Louvre with me today.*

Sorry, I wrote. *Wish I was there.* And then, as an

afterthought, another message, a few minutes later, *It was beautiful at the farm today.*

He didn't understand why I wouldn't go. I wanted to see France, to dine in Paris, to drive a little car through the countryside and marvel in vast museums. How could I be in two places at once though? I'd imagine drifting through the Louvre; I'd ghost myself into his travels, trying the experiences on like new dresses, but it was just pretending. I knew my place. Not being able to take the trip didn't hurt badly; it ached, like a day-old bee sting.

I didn't know it at the time but he'd started experimenting with new drugs, nitrous and pills and who-knows-what in Europe and they'd strung his thoughts out in long lines like Christmas lights, blinking red, then green, then blue. He'd shown up, drunk and a complete mess at our friend's wedding in England.

She'd written me, thanking me for the gift I'd sent from the both of us, saying, *Jayden has lost his innocent appeal.*

"Don't you feel like you're missing out?" Jayden asked during brief phone calls. He'd dial, drunk, from the other side of the ocean and I would pick up, heavy with exhaustion and try to make sense of our two days. I kept a picture of him by my bedside so I could look at it and better imagine him because as we talked it was hard to make out the boy I'd loved from the guy I was being woken by at dusk Paris time, as dawn was breaking on my side of the world.

I also kept a photo of the field crew from Cedar Circle on my desk. It was my favorite picture of myself, as if this image captured exactly what I wanted the lens of the world to see. In it, I am sitting in the bed of a truck and its carriage has settled low under the onions stacked high behind me. It was the biggest onion harvest the crew had seen, and we are all grinning, holding up huge onions with the greens limp and brown. In the picture, I am resting my hands on the warm body of the truck. My smile is real and raising dimples in my cheeks, my hair is messy but pretty and I am not posing, just sitting, with my feet dangling off the tailgate. From where the truck is parked, I can look out beyond the camera to the fields in full bloom, high in mid-summer growth and almost see the river between the shore and the rise of New Hampshire into wooded hills and place myself exactly in the landscape.

"Hello?" I'd stammer, looking between the picture of me on the truck and the picture of Jayden. He'd call from friend's phones, hotel lobbies, and with phone cards so the number appeared mysterious and long on my screen.

"It's me, Megan. Jesus. Don't you recognize my voice?" Jayden would tell me what I missed out on, listing his day's routine.

Maybe it was the exhaustion that robbed me of words but I couldn't express to him on the phone why seeing the plants each day as they grew meant so much to me, or what a paycheck bought me—not just food and rent, but freedom. Harvesting in the fog, planting and weeding in the heat of the afternoons, driving the old farm trucks, licking the tip of a lime wedged in the throat of a cold Corona while my dirty legs dangled in river water, listening to thunder crack the air above the barn, that was my poetry. I could taste it, dust it from my skin, and smell it under my fingernails.

On the mantel in the apartment in Oregon, I kept a vintage letterpress alphabet, each shape reversed in relief. The metal letters were sharp and hard, the forms blackened by ink. I could feel the hard edges of 'A' and the soft, infinite 'O'. The farm's poetry was like those letters, so utilitarian and tangible that I could read it blind.

When he flew back from Paris, I'd been waiting for him at the airport. My skin was deeply tanned from working all summer in the fields and I was surprised by how fair he was. His light cheeks were patterned with freckles, his auburn curls kissed with blond. He'd stumbled off the flight, a little drunk, holding his low back where the pain radiated, he'd tell me later in the car. A pain that he was trying to figure out how to cure. At the moment, the only way to ease it was through drinking. He'd seen a doctor in Paris, he promised me, who said that it would heal on its own. He just had to rest. I'd packed him a homemade dinner of fresh tomatoes from the farm, roasted corn, grilled chicken speckled with cilantro I'd picked that morning. The smell of it filled the car as I drove him back to my parents' home, feeling only partially complete. We held hands quietly in the dark. Somehow, despite six weeks of separation, we had little to say to each other. In bed, we were strangers too. His back hurt, he said, and he was tired from the flight. We held each other but when sleep overcame us, we drifted apart.

The cabin seemed like our last chance but the night's fight had ruined it. Or else made it so messy that I didn't know where to begin picking up the pieces. I was embarrassed by my tears and our sloppy shouting match. It didn't seem like the way to end something which had once meant the world to me. As we packed up and scrubbed our dinner dishes clean, we moved through a pressing, easy silence. Maybe we'd said everything we needed to already. Maybe the condom, which Jayden had thrown dramatically into the trash the night before, had done all of it for us. "There," he'd shouted, "are you happy now?"

I wasn't happy. My body was sick and felt out of place. In the clean light of that morning in the mountains, I bumped into things, struggled to fit into my clothing, forgot how to tie my hair up and seemed unable to live within the husk of my skin.

"What's wrong with me?" I asked Jayden, after I jabbed my mascara brush onto my cheek, leaving a black smear of makeup.

"We need to eat something," he said. "And get coffee." He threw the backpack over his shoulder. "Ready?"

I wiped my cheek with a piece of toilet paper. In the mirror, I looked hazy, more like an apparition than a body. I lifted the bags of our trash-empty tequila bottles, leftover spaghetti, an unopened condom, and my stomach churned imagining the contents. I'd considered myself a morning person even before working at the farm, but I wanted to skip over that morning as if it were a bad song.

As we drove out of the woods my insides felt parched and empty but good, like a rag wrung out and sundried on the line. We stopped for breakfast at a diner in a

small town, the sort of place with four stores along a
straight Main Street. It was a brilliant, clean morning
with the flavor of fall in the air and the town glowing
crisp and bright. I felt I had to capture every moment
of that morning, trapped in the amber of time. I still
remember it perfectly, like an awakening. I can hear the
folding and rustling of the old men's newspapers at the
diner's counter and the rattle of rusty pickup trucks on
the streets. Everyone looked up when we walked in and
smiled big, kind smiles. They must have been thinking of themselves when they were young lovers. I was
wearing a cotton sundress and espadrilles; Jayden was in
sweatpants and a soccer jersey, his curls rolling long on
his neck.

The raspberries in the pancakes I ordered were tart
and fresh, picked, I imagined, from the owner's backyard, off rambling wild bushes. The syrup was real
maple, the good clear amber made from old trees, and
it flooded into the little craters on the pancake's surface left by the cooked berries. My mug of tea steamed
around my face and I felt its warmth and moisture as
daylight broke over the buildings on the other side of
the street and lit on the dew dropping off the town's
iron lampposts. I looked over the table at Jayden. He'd
kept his dark sunglasses on and was scowling at the
old-timers, the worn plastic plate and the overstuffed
omelet he'd ordered.

"They shouldn't be allowed to call this an omelet," he
muttered, poking his fork at the fold of yellow eggs bulg-
ing with local cheddar, onions and crisp green peppers.

He puckered his lips at the black coffee and then pushed it far away from him, over to my side of the table, as if in its commonness, it belonged with me.

That morning I knew I had grown up as much as we had grown apart. The pull we'd felt when he was in Paris was a symptom but not the problem. I realized over my pancakes that we wanted vastly different lives. We weren't us anymore. The fatality of that statement had been hovering over us for weeks but pulling it down into words reduced it somehow into something hard and easy to handle, like a stone. It had a weight to it, like rocks in the pocket of a suicide, a heavy sense of doom. But the feeling was breaking over us now and the only way past it was to live in it. That doom was a fear of things to come. It was the sense of an early end, like a summer that dies cold.

⸙

I cup each tomato in my palm, give it a little squeeze, and then twist it from the stem. With my thumbnail, I dig out the calyx and stem and place the tomato blossom-side up in a black crate, one at a time, like precious gems. My sweat runs clear through green pollen dust, but my armpits seemed to absorb the stuff so that even on days when I don't pick tomatoes my shirts are stained neon green under the arms. Nothing, not even bleach, removes the mark of those plants.

The farm stand is filled to overflowing with tomatoes. The kitchen staff boils and chops as much as they can but we can't get them all off the farm before they soften and turn to mush. I find a book that Justin, who once tended the tomatoes with great tenderness and scholarly attention to detail, left in The Yellow House about heirloom varieties and take it home with me one night in my backpack. It shows page after page of fruit clusters, the tomato split and displayed for the camera like jewelry, with the seeds shining golden and the flesh brightly colored. Beside the photos are descriptions of flavors, and a long paragraph charting the history of the variety, where it was grown, when it was discovered and why it is worth the space it fills out hungrily as it sprawls.

The heirlooms varieties are my favorites to pick; they are strange and shy and hard to harvest. Some of them hide deep in the heart of the plant and have to be extracted like a surgeon working through bone and muscle. Others ripen to greens and yellows that to the eye look under-ripe so every fruit has to be felt, carefully, before it is plucked. Some of the larger varieties, called beefsteaks, can split overnight, their flesh swelled by changes in the groundwater deep under the surface where the long tips of the white roots drink. A rainstorm can make all the ripe fruit expand and shatter, the skin drawing back and cracking like fault lines. To pick these I have to know the weather, the watering cycle of the tomatoes, how quickly they will ripen off the vine, how hot the barn is, and how quickly they might sell. I have to be a future-teller to harvest heirloom tomatoes.

They have names that are like characters from children's books: Aunt Ginny's Purple, Black Prince, Silvery

Fir Tree. Others bear the landmarks of the places where they were first cultivated, connecting the plants I harvest back into other lands, other growing spaces. There's Cherokee Purple from the state of Georgia, Striped German from Bavaria, and the black tomatoes from the Crimea—Black from Tula and Black Krim. The fruit is as varied and colorful as their names—jewel-toned, a rainbow from white to green, yellow, orange, pink, red, striped, purple and deep brown. Some are the size of quail eggs, while others are the size of grapefruits.

At the farmers market I set up a name card with each variety which contains a brief description, like the information in Justin's book, about their flavor. I bring a cutting board and knife and dice up ripe fruit for sampling. I set a small plate in front of each row of tomatoes and display them like a rainbow, the flesh glistening in the morning sun, starting with the greens and ending with the blacks and purples. The shift of colors is eye-catching and customers stop and walk the length of the table, reading the names out loud to each other, spearing samples on toothpicks and rolling the fruit in their mouths like wine. The green tomatoes are bright and low in acid, their flavor is citrusy while the reds and pinks are sweet and well balanced. The dark tomatoes are very acidic, almost salty, and when the weather has been perfect, hot and dry, they develop an almost earthy flavor. Robert and I hand customers a bag and they fill it with one tomato from each row. The colors swell against the clear plastic.

In the history of tomatoes, I can't help but see the

greater patterns of homecoming. Their story is circular. The plant grows wild in the mountains of central Mexico. There it is a bushy, leggy thing with fruit that is slightly fuzzy and orange. The Spanish called it *tomate*, their pronunciation of the Aztec *tomatl*. When it was first brought back to Europe it was regarded as a poison, since the leaves of the tomato so closely resembled those of the European plant, deadly nightshade. Carolus Linnaeus, the father of scientific classification, gave the tomato the Latin name *Solanum lycopersicum*, the latter of which translates to "wolf peach." Wolf, because the deadly nightshade was associated with the magic of werewolves and witches, and peach because the fruit was then still fuzzy and orange. Ornamental tomatoes spread around Europe but were never highly prized like the tulip was. Once they were introduced into peasant gardens, most likely by laborers in an aristocrat's display gardens, they stayed in that community for hundreds of years, developing regional mutations which forever altered what we think of as the tomato. These growers saved their seed, season after season, in their small cottage plots.

It was this pattern of seed saving and home consumption that allowed the tomato to diversify. Tomatoes mutate naturally but they can also be deliberately cross-pollinated to create hybrids. So, if a gardener touched the flowers of two different plants together, he might create a unique variety, which over the course of several years, stabilized and became a new type of tomato. Natural mutants might also have been saved because they were so surprising—beautiful mysteries in the familiar garden growth, and their stock, too, became the seed that is now cultivated.

Fuzzy, small, orange tomatoes were brought to Europe in the mid-1500s and by the mid-1800s the fruit had developed in regional pockets, into brown, red, pink, yellow and striped colors; into taper, ox-heart, round, cherry, and paste shapes. When immigrants crossed the Atlantic, they brought their heirloom seeds with them and in the gardens of America new varieties bloomed, pinks and purples, the sweet Brandywines of Pennsylvania, Cherokee Purple of Georgia. By the time the tomato returned to the continent of its origin it had shifted, shaped by chance and by the hands of generations of farmers.

But it isn't only this circular history that draws me to them, the beauty of a family hiding seeds in their steamer luggage, the wild poetry of genetic mutation. It is their colors and their shapes. I can taste sun and soil and water in them, a balance of acid and sugar. They can be sliced up and served like cuts of steak, lightly salted and drizzled in green extra virgin olive oil or eaten whole, like peaches or apples. They are the jewels of August, just as strawberries are to June. And like the berries, I am woven into their story through my labor, through the crew's careful pruning and trellising, through my watchful harvest. I feel every tomato before I pick them, their skin slick and slightly fuzzy with pollen. I lay each fruit in the crate like a huge ruby or emerald. I know them as seeds in my palm, poured from their packet, then later as tiny arching seedlings in their neat germination flats, then finally as tall, draping plants, shading out the bright fruit in their hearts.

Inside the flesh, in the brilliant gems of their interior chambers, packed tightly around the raw, slick seeds, they contain all those memories of my labor, as well as the sunlight of every day, the huge night sky that is unknown to me, the rain from each storm felt on my skin also, dew from summer dawn's rising, nitrogen alchemized from lightning strikes and clover roots, groundwater from the basement of the land, and water from the slow, brown Connecticut River.

CHAPTER FOUR

The stereo played our favorite songs like a soundtrack to the past. As we drove the windows opened to the buzzing rush of August air. Behind my sunglasses, my hangover faded to a pleasant fog which distorted heartbreak into something like a pleasant ache in my chest. Jayden sang along to words we'd heard a thousand times before—Dylan, Springsteen, Cash—mouthing the lyrics like small prayers. Along the roadside yellow goldenrod and bright purple asters clustered and swayed in the wake of passing cars. The season was rushing forward and so were we. I put my legs up on the dashboard and examined the dirt still crusted in my kneecaps and toenails. Sunlight bathed my skin brown. Somehow, we were moving out of what we had been and it didn't hurt too bad. Maybe, I thought, smiling, we were flowing towards something, not away. Music filled my head like honey bees, sweet with the dusty pollen of nostalgia.

A few hours into our drive we stopped at a roadside attraction which had been advertising itself for miles on tall, hand-painted billboards. This land was empty beneath us, the soil honeycombed by vast caves that had become tourist traps, gaudy with mid-century branding. Although Jayden and I were both sweating and slightly sick to our stomachs, we wanted to do something like we would have before all of our fighting, the distance, the bitterness. These places had always been our portals to the odd and beautiful, trips that could have become poetry but never did. In the parking lot families rushed children out of vans while we sucked down the last of our smokes. Something in the scene was off. Maybe it was the hangover, I thought. We were hunting for charged irony, for subtle humor, but at Howe Caverns the air was flat and the oddity we were searching for seemed only like the ordinary beauty of the everyday.

Jayden tried, at first, to whisper commentary during a boat ride through the limestone cavern's river, water dripping, slow and bored, in illuminated spotlights. We sat together on a damp bench, shoulder to shoulder with kids in rain slickers and families snapping pictures of the monsters made of melted stone. He muttered about the people around us, about the cheap plastic boat, the corny names of the rock formations, but really it was all too easy. I found him childish and put my finger over my lips, trying to quiet him. At the Bridal Altar, he fell silent. Stepping off the boat, I followed his shape as our tour drifted towards a large heart, cut into the floor of the cave and lit from below so that it glowed, scuffed and sour-candy pink under the water shoes of tourists. The guide echoed on about luck in love, about the cave's owner staging his daughter's wedding down here in the dripping dark. And in groups of two, siblings hugging, partners holding hands, he took pictures of each duo over the glowing heart. The flash exploded my vision into black fireworks.

When it was our turn to stand on the heart, I looked to my side for Jayden but he wasn't there. I moved away, into the shadows at the edge of the cave's chamber and let the family behind me spill onto its lighted face. I stood on a rock ledge and peered over the crowd and then out past them, into the river of dark water.

"Jayden?" I whispered. The guide pressed on ahead, his flashlight bobbing across the ceiling. "Jayden?"

The space around me became dim. I watched the backs of the tour group as they shuffled along the wet floor toward the light. Jayden slipped out of the shadows in an alcove above the Bridal Altar, his hands deep in his pockets, his head low like it weighed too much for his neck.

He didn't try to find me, he just drifted into the crowd. I rushed to him and caught his hand. It was clammy and cold as stone.

We followed the guide in silence through the rest of the limestone rooms. There were possible routes forward but neither of us took them. We let each potential conversation slip away like dripping water, rolling off our lips.

Upstairs in the gift shop, we bought sandwiches and sodas and two geodes the size of baseballs. With tiny rock hammers, we cracked open the stones and each snapped into perfect cross-sections, glittering with white crystals.

We wrapped our broken stones in tissue paper and opened our sandwiches on a picnic table outside on the vast lawn above the caverns. The August sun beat down and even under dark glasses our eyes throbbed. Everyone around us seemed to be having a nice day. We were the only ones suffering. Usually, this would have made me feel more honest but I felt ashamed instead and kept my eyes on the cold, stale sandwich.

Back in the car, as Jayden pulled onto the interstate towards home, I unwrapped my geode and lost myself in its snow-white center, where the crystals turned to peaks around the core of open air. It looked like a seed, but in reverse, I thought, growing on the inside instead of blooming out and up. I fit it back together to form an ordinary rock ball then opened it again into shimmering husks. Two halves of the same thing. We are not the same person, I thought. It seemed simple enough but our love was founded on similarity. I wondered if I fought hard enough if I could fuse us back together like the geode before the hammer split its crystals.

As the caves receded into the shadow of the forest and the road opened clear ahead of us, I leaned my cheek on the cool glass of the window. Jayden slipped a pair of dark sunglasses over his aching eyes and I closed mine, heavy, against the light breaking through the windshield.

By August at the farm, my days are tidal.

The world around me is expanding. For the first time since I was a little girl, I feel connected to a specific place. A place I know like the back of my own hand. This knowledge is like love; it draws me closer to the barn, the greenhouse, the roads, the soil, and the fields. I know the crew too, so well that I can often guess what they will say and when, in a story, they will laugh.

So, like Alice in Wonderland, I grow and shrink, grow and shrink each day.

When I am very large, very aware, I feel I understand more than I ever have. I can see for miles, I think, like a bird looking down on the landscape, the fields just quilts of green against the blue-brown ribbon of the river. I can see myself too, at the farm, with my sharpened harvesting knife, my pink bikini flashing against the rows, my skin tanned the color of the dust.

I'm eighteen when I first I feel this expansion. The world opens like a book for me. That season the farm grows with an energy that justifies all of our love and labor. Soil, like a body, slowly leeches out poisons until it is clean again. Time, water cycles, harvests, all these things remove chemicals and allow the farm, after three years of work, to finally earn the right to market our products as certified organic. An inspector walks all the edges of the farm with a clipboard and looks through the files in the office, checking off boxes on our application form.

When the state mails us our official organic seal, I tape a copy of it up on the legs of the market tent so that everyone can note this achievement. Although the vegetables and fruits I've been growing and selling were produced using organic methods, now we can market them as certified. Three years of work have paid off. I imagine the fields like a woman, cared for, treated with love, nursed back to health with warm broths and herbal tea until her hair is lush and shining and her skin clear and bright. I think sometimes of myself as this woman and wonder when I will be so transformed. I look in the mirror, hoping to see a girl with no darkness in the pits of her eyes, no shadows like strings binding her to the past.

The fields grow rich and bright that season. Will, the farm's owner, reaches into the dark silt and draws up a handful of it. As it crumbles and cakes, he describes all the little bugs and creatures in it, a dynamic universe too small to see that turns the dead into food for the living. He pulls up a long root of white clover and points to white clusters, tiny bubbles that hang from hair-like fibers. Solid nitrogen, he explains, fixed by the plant itself, gathered from the soil and air and made soluble in the soil.

Under me the world grows, populated by microbes and worms, chemistry and the rolling, digesting bodies of dead plants and little creatures being reborn again as corn stalks and tomatoes. Will tells the crew that the real value of the farm lies in the soil, not in the crops we harvest each season. I imagine those open, blank fields of spring, like all the pages I will ever write.

That summer is huge; I watch the sky and clouds and feel the vastness of the world. I think about how ancient water is, caught up the cycle of transformation. When thunderheads roll over the fields, I imagine their molecules in the nostrils of mammoths, or the throats of ancient Egyptians, and feel woven into a landscape that is bigger than my story. It is all there, on the land. I brush my hands over the broad leaves of kale and they shake with wonder at the process of photosynthesis. What a marvel that plants live off the light of a star.

Our conversations that summer are expansive as if the success of the season elevated our dialogue. One day I am weeding strawberries with my friend Justin. It is just the two of us and the task is huge, so we break it up into small victories. We finish a row and then stop and smoke a cigarette. Shadows rotate around us as we weed, the day thinning away as we pull and tear and establish strawberry runners in the soft nest of soil and straw. Noon light shifts into the late afternoon. The sun moves from one shoulder to the other like a warm hand.

At the end of a row we lie down in the tall grass and look up at the sky. We might be the only people on Earth that day. There is no sound, just the buzzing of insects and our own close breath. Above us hang the curling branches of honey locusts that bloom white and sweet and cover the fields with blossoms like June snow. It's a clear day; the sky is light blue as if most of the color has burned out of it. Clouds move along steadily, so thin they cast no shadow when they pass over the face of the sun. High above a turkey vulture spins in concentric circles, focusing on the smell of death somewhere in the hayfield to the north.

Justin asks me what I see. I pause and look up into the pale dome of the sky. I tell him about the trees and the clouds, the sun and the birds. We are smoking his

Pall Malls. We suck on them between sentences and the smoke seems to rise like words in that silence.

"What if we don't see the same thing?" he asks, "what if your sky and my sky are different? What if our trees and birds aren't the same?"

I wonder why they would be different.

He says he grew up in a different home, has read different books, is a man . . . maybe these differences shape our perceptions, maybe we know the names of rough shapes, like bird and tree, but actually see very different things. I stay quiet. I know that Justin's philosophical mind works far out in theoretical regions which I can hardly grasp but I say that I think that the birds and trees and clouds are probably all the same. They are the things that are always true. It's just people who get things wrong.

He says that the world is full of shadows. Projections that distract us. The grass is blowing around our faces. When I look over, I see him staring up at the sky, the sun passing over his dark brown eyes. He is talking to it, as much as he is to me. The words are going up and joining the vapors and bugs and water molecules that rise and move beyond the farm.

CHAPTER FIVE

When Jayden and I returned from the Catskills we slunked upstairs to my bedroom and lay in my double bed, as far apart as two bodies could, touching only at the hip and shoulder. Without speaking we both decided to treat each other like friends, especially in the company of others. It was as if we were incapable of describing our split, the break in the rock that had opened us to the possibility of separate lives. We continued on through the planned course of our time together. Paris, the cabin and the caves grew small behind us. We moved forward with neither enthusiasm nor hesitation. We'd set ourselves up on this course for so long that no amount of rage or sorrow seemed capable of knocking one of us off. In bed I looked to my right and saw Jayden's picture hanging there, reminding me of the boy I had once been in love with.

Early in the morning, a day after we returned from New York, we rose with my family and packed into our minivan for a day in Boston. I didn't want to go but I didn't want to stay either, stuck in the silence of the house with only each other for company. Proceeding felt better than retreating into what we'd left in that cabin, empty bottles and eyes burnt red. The car was silent and the day dawned hot along the interstate, reflecting off glass skyscrapers and blinding fields of windshields. Although Jayden and I hadn't had a drop to drink my head was muddled and my eyes still felt swollen. I wore sunglasses at dawn.

By the time we reached Logan Airport the day was loud and bright—a buzzing, angry thing like bees about to move hives. Jayden and I stood together with my family in a security line, waiting to hug goodbye to my brother as he checked into his first international flight. We'd come to see him off and to spend the rest of the day shopping on Market Street, eating lobster rolls and walking the cobblestones. I held Jayden's hand loosely and felt his height and warmth against me. It would be so much easier to pretend that it was alright between us. To go into the school year as lovers. How would we fit in the apartment, I wondered, how could we divide a car, a television set, a cat? I'd been working these calculations all morning, trying to find equity in our separation but coming up with unbalanced scales. No matter how I worked it we both lost by breaking apart or staying together.

Jayden had been irritated since we woke. "It's my back," he'd said when I asked, but I knew that it was more than that. He was itching to leave me. Desperate to get back to where he called home. It was always harder for him to pretend that we could make it right. I was the one who could make-believe things into new forms, growing like the fruit of a strange seed. A small- town Yankee into a Valley Girl. A farmer into a poet. Two broken hearts into one healthy organ. I did this work, growing better tomorrows, because I couldn't make sense of my place without him. All of my futures had Jayden like a compass needle, pointing forward and up. He was my lodestone.

As the crowd tightened around us, my parents started to list off travel tips to my brother. How he should behave in the customs line, what foods he should avoid, how much water he should try to drink and from what sources. Both relative homebodies who preferred their rural home over exotic destinations, my father and mother repeated what I assumed they'd heard from friends, or in travel magazines in their dentist's office. Jayden jumped in, shouting, his face red, ticking off his own ideas about how a young man should travel abroad. My brother stood blankly, burdened with luggage. Jayden leaned in over the ropes and I saw my brother pull back, confused. I stood back, behind my sisters, unable to make sense of the charge that had just taken place in the boy I had once loved. Jayden countered my father's advice and laid out his own mantras about security lines, packing, and how to carry a passport. Every time my parents tried to get in a word over him, he stepped on their lines. They all got louder and louder until suddenly he was yelling and my mother was cursing him, calling him *ungrateful* while he was shouting *you're a fucking bitch* and then my brother was at the head of the line and he waved and pushed through security and my parents stopped fighting with Jayden and rushed to my brother, blowing kisses. By the time my mother and father turned around from his departure, Jayden had stormed away. I watched him rush through the pack of bodies around the security check-point and then keep walking until he was washed into the sea of the crowd.

I looked towards where he'd disappeared and then back at my family. I tried to read their reactions but the whole scene was rushed and hazy. We so rarely raised our voices that I didn't know how any of us would respond. My mother's face was red and she was shaking with rage. My father was breathing like he'd taught me to breathe when I was having asthma attacks as a girl, sucking in deeply, holding the air in, then slowly, on a count of 1-2-3, releasing. My older sister, Elise, asked if we could still go shopping. Hannah, my youngest sister, was wide-eyed with terror. Our family never shouted. When my parents were angry, they spoke to each other alone in their room. Or my father called a family meeting and presented three-point problems to us like he was selling software. In contrast, Jayden's family yelled and screamed, tried to burn a house down during a divorce, took each other to court, and left long, irate voicemails years after their set-tlement. His yelling horrified my family. They'd tolerated his "California lifestyle" well enough for four years but had always commented, under their breath, about the drugs, the temper, the late nights. I knew they had done everything they could to welcome him but would never really accept him. There was no way to braid him into the fabric of their steady, hard-working, scheduled lives.

"Leave him," my mother said flatly. "Good riddance."

My father tried to console me. "She can't just leave him here." To which my mother threw her hands up in the air and turned towards the hot glare of the summer afternoon, blazing beyond banks of glass doors.

My sister asked again about shopping and my mother promised over her shoulder that they'd swing back through the airport later to pick Jayden up.

Through all of their noise, I stood still, like an island in a river. Everything flowed around me but nothing really touched me. I felt as separate from my family as I did from Jayden. I was embarrassed, too, in a way that burned hotter than my anger toward him or than my shame at our fight in the cabin. I didn't want to be connected to him—to this loud, angry person—and yet I felt the cold circle of the engagement ring on my finger. I was still his. Or he was mine. I didn't know which. As the loudspeakers echoed their announcements and rolling bags clicked over the tiles, I stood frozen. My mouth was slightly open.

"Megan, we're leaving," my mom said. She touched the bare skin of my arm and snapped me back to the cold tile and hot sunlight. "We'll come back later and pick you up."

"I've got to find him," I stammered. "He's not well," I added. "His back…"

"We understand," my father said softly, his face still moon-white with shock. "You can come with us, too, honey if you'd like."

"No," I said, pushing out of their circle and into the rush of the concourse. "No. I've got to find him." I slung my purse behind my back and started walking as fast as I could without breaking into a run. My heart was pounding, *boom, boom* through my skull like incoming thunder and the whole place melted away, all the people faded, the crowds became ghost-thin, invisible. There was only the slap of my sandals on the tiles and Jayden, somewhere in the twisting hallways of the airport. He didn't have his wallet. Was he even wearing shoes, I wondered? Worry washed over me, a worry that smothered the heat of my shame. I had to find him, I told myself, rushing from terminal to terminal.

I'd been his mother before when he was sick, or drunk, or high. Once he'd stood all night weeping and petting the nose of a white mare who'd walked up to the fence line along a canyon road in Malibu. She'd come in the bright moonlight to his hand. I'd sat cross-legged on the gravel as it cooled and led him back at dawn, barefoot, to bed. I could take care of him again. Helping was at least something, some form of love. Maybe that was where we grew from again, maybe that was what brought us together. I knew how to tend something—my hands, calloused and dark, were the hands of a farmer. I could string up, water, fertilize. I could grow something from seed to fruit. Maybe I could make him better? Maybe I could heal his pain and he'd transform for me as I had for him.

I was stopped twice by security before I finally found Jayden, hunched on a bench, staring blankly at the floor. He was four terminals away from where we'd said goodbye to my brother. Sitting there, with no bag, no books, he looked so lonely, like a man with nothing to lose.

I was breathing hard when I said his name.

He looked up at me with his big green eyes and I knew he was sorry. Everything was drained out of him like the clouds after a storm.

"Send my stuff home to me, OK?" He said.

"You're leaving? You don't have your wallet. Your bags are at my house."

"I called my mom. They're paying extra for my ticket."

"Now?" I sat beside him on the bench. The airport settled around us, people appeared, noises rose again, light cut through the huge glass windows.

"I'll see you in Portland," he said, standing up.

"Jayden. . ." I reached for his hand but he stepped away as if drawn forward by a string.

"We'll figure it out then." He waved and stepped into the flood of a security line, clutching his ticket.

I watched his back fade into the crowd. His broad shoulders and slim waist. I wanted to rest my cheek on his shoulder blade and as much as I tried I couldn't remember the way his skin smelled. Already, that memory had flown away. I was tired and footsore from running and I sat hunched on the bench, as Jayden had just rested, my arms hanging heavy on my knees, my hair flowing over my cheeks. It felt so hard to move forward. Couldn't we just go back instead? To the place where we'd listened to coyotes up the canyon in L.A., drinking raspberry vodka and shouting poetry back up at the pack? Couldn't we go back to our first year in Portland, to the promise that that apartment held, those afternoons in the home improvement stores, those first nights of takeout and watching the city's lights like a bright blanket spread through the valley? I wondered if I could be that girl again. I didn't know what we'd be able to figure out in Portland.

Without Jayden, the future seemed as boundless as a day in the summer. It stretched and stretched into shimmering heat. Empty but beautiful. I'd always wanted meaning, things to give weight and hold me down. I'd felt often that our love was meaningful. But it was so bitter a taste in my mouth. I remembered the cabin, his exchange with my parents, his voice sharp on the phone. I wanted to clean out the sourness. I wanted to lay something sweet on my tongue and let it dissolve. Corn, watermelon, berry. Sunlight fell on my skin and the smell of sweat and salt rose from my body.

Jayden was gone. I stood up and walked out of the airport, feeling as if I'd left something of myself behind. Like lost luggage I imagined our relationship waiting endlessly in the airport to be claimed and returned to its rightful place. As I sat outside the terminal waiting for my family to return, I watched planes break off the ground and rise over the bay. I wondered which one Jayden was on and if he was sitting near the window and could see the city shrinking beneath the wings. I hoped he was feeling as lost as I was but had the feeling that he was flying home toward something and I was being left behind.

My map of the farm starts at the beginning of time. Ancient truth anchors the fields, forged from elements older than the earth—stardust, ice from deadly comets, minerals crushed in crucibles of great explosions at the beginning of time. Spinning hardened these materials. They were opened by fire and raised by water until they sprouted and grew blue-green and round as a river stone. These ingredients are mixed into soil, so that with dirty hands, and soil under my fingernails, I reach back to the oldest story, the story of creation.

Above the farm lays the flat lake of sky. A brown river snakes to the east, draining slowly from the cold northern lakes on the border of Canada. To the west, hills rise steadily into the Green Mountains. On a map Cedar Circle sits in the middle of New Hampshire and Vermont, those two states cradle together like lovers holding each other through a winter's night. The soil there feels fine as the skin on the inside of a girl's thigh, agronomists call it "sandy loam." The air smells like sweet berries, cut grass, and straw dust, brown water, pine needles, and railroad metal. Compass directions run through the valley so perfectly that I can use the land to locate myself, reading the river as a north-south axis and the sun's path as map points.

Cedar Circle's fields spread out on the banks of the Connecticut River. Across those steady brown waters in New Hampshire, the land falls straight into the river, barely contained by white pine and oak roots. On the Vermont side great floods in unrecorded time smoothed and flattened the land into formations called "intervales." Once, the current had run all the way to the granite cliffs, but that had been before humans lived in the valley and only the shape of the ground remembered that surge and

spill. Before the floods, the basement of a great glacier
had carved the land, ground huge volcanic peaks down
to their cooled lava chambers of glittering granite and
formed the bare summits of the Appalachian Mountains.
The ice etched deep lakes that filled with snowmelt and
sliced through new valleys making rivers, streams and
brook beds. I like to close my eyes and imagine time on
fast-forward, the land changing like the fields through the
cycles of seasons.

The farmland is smooth and polished by the ages. All
of the lines have been softened, the edges rubbed out.
Hills slip into water, river banks roll into fields. Only
modern transportation arteries cut hard lines through
the landscape. To the west, the state highway, Pavillion
Road and railroad tracks border the farm, so the property sits inside them like a secret garden. The river forms
the eastern border—more sinuous, flowing in gentle
curves down to the ocean so the farm feels contained.
But overhead the sky has no end; it rolls above roads,
hedgerows, treetops and telephone poles, carrying
clouds from the west.

Cedar Circle is a collection of three properties,
quilted together up the central riverbank. The Home
Farm spreads over a broad twenty acres from Pavillion
Road to the river. An old red dairy barn, which sits in the
middle of the yard, functions as the heart of the farm.
From it, seeds go out and crops return to be stored. The
crew hangs their coats in its dim chill at dawn, and leans
against its boards, soaking up the last heat of the day at
sunset. Under its stone foundation generations of skunks

hibernate and litters of kittens are born. In the rafters of what was once the hayloft, black bats and soft, grey pigeons roost in the constant twilight beneath the roof. The barn holds our tools, oiled and organized, sharpened with a spark from the worn wetstones. In the fall and winter, it stores root crops against the cold.

I always sense ghosts there, familiar, almost like specters of the crew I work with during the day. Palm grease and summer sweat from the hands of the old farmers has smoothed the wood on the walls. Long-dead horses nibbled at the edges of the stalls, leaving only the memory of their teeth marking their stay in the place. Every corner has been touched so that, like the land, it is polished by contact with time. Our workdays begin and end in the barn. Light falls through the shrinking sideboards and cuts through the dusty air in warm, golden slivers, shifting as the day turns. Night in the barn fades darker than beneath the sky. Each year the roofline slants more until it forms a gentle spinal arch, like the back of a reclining girl, silhouetted against the clarity of sunrise that breaks against its broad eastern wall.

Four greenhouses open facing the barn. With their high, arched metal ribs and plastic skins, they reminded me of the bodies of whales. As soon as I walk into one the air changes and becomes heavy with moisture. In the summer, the greenhouses are bright with flowers and smell like geranium leaves and sticky petunias, wet compost and blood-meal fertilizer that give the soil a metallic tang, like the taste of biting your tongue.

Between the greenhouses, the farm stand greets the

road with its two big garage doors slung up, welcoming customers into the shade. Sometimes the place vibrates, busy and loud with shoppers and their children, the parking lot packed with cars, the greenhouses filled with gardeners, the lawn covered with picnic blankets and half-naked babies stained with berry juice. But, on rainy days, or in the slow seasons, the farm stand is a hollow place, a cavity of sound and movement. Itchi, the farm cat, usually shy around people, slinks in and sleeps near the space heater behind the counter.

The property has two farmhouses, one white and the other yellow, and we call them The White House and The Yellow House. The White House had been divided, years ago, into two apartments for staff. It sits across from the farm stand, and although the windows are heavily curtained and blocked in summer by an ancient lilac, it is always a public place. People move in and out of it, collecting memories of parties and nights on the porch, counting hours in cigarettes, stargazing above the cornfields, watching tail lights travel down the pinprick of Pavilion Road's terminating point. It smells like sweat and soil, leather gloves, charcoal smoke and sticky sweet beer. The owners of the farm live in The Yellow House across the broad lawn, behind the shade of a huge maple tree. Ivy climbs its chimney and then makes a dive down the brick. Like many old houses, the floors have a tilt to them so that walking them you feel as if you are on a boat at sea, rolling through swells. Peeling wallpaper lines the walls of its small rooms, printed with tiny flowers and vines. The smell of the dirt and stone basement come up through the heat vents. Rats and squirrels run through the walls so that I always feel surrounded there by something living and breathing.

Down by the river, a small cabin sits in the shade of the hedgerow, cluttered with kayaks and life vests. We rest under the eaves on a collection of battered wicker furniture at the end of each summer day. A fire pit lays near the riverbank, encircled by rotting Adirondack chairs and tree-stump stools. Between two big spruce trees, a dock steps out into the water, just far enough out into the brown current to dive from. We spend our summer nights down there, drinking away sunsets, starting fires with wooden produce boxes and rotting pine logs, shooting off fireworks to celebrate birthdays, harvests, and the 4th of July, and swimming in water which reflects the stars.

At the southern end of Pavillion Road, near where it meets up again with the state highway, Cedar Circle rents two acres of blueberries and an overgrown asparagus patch where the ferns grew eight feet tall above high grass. In the high summer, when the bushes are thick with leaves and the weight of silver-blue fruit pulls each cane down to the earth, I like to hide out there, filling pint after pint in privacy.

The final property spills out behind a red barn, boarded off and full of feral cats, a little way down the state highway. Pumpkins, sweet corn, potatoes, winter squash, and straw grow there, slightly untended, always a bit wilder than the crops at the home farm. Long ago a house had perched on the highest point of the field and its bricks are churned up under the blades of plows and cultivators like old bones. From its site I can see upriver to the broad face of Holt's Ledge and down towards Hanover. I know the land so well, like the body of a lover, like my own skin.

Maybe that's why my heart aches so terribly for the touch of river silt and the cool air in the barn and the flex of my muscle as I grip the handle of my hoe upon which I carved the words, "this machine kills fascists." I picture myself against the map of the farm: ragged cutoff blue jean shorts, a pink bikini top, a paisley scarf wrapped around my dark hair, chunky sunglasses like a celebrity just out of rehab and a dirty pair of steel-toed boots which my mother calls *shit kickers* and which I am forbidden to wear inside our house. Dirt stains my kneecaps and the lines of my palms. There are Band-Aids on my fingers from knife cuts and I wear a deep, dirty tan. I resemble a pirate princess mixed with a punk rocker. This is the uniform of a farm girl.

CHAPTER SIX

After Jayden left I spent my time at the farm with my head down in the rows, avoiding the crew's gaze, trying to ignore the ache in my chest and the stone in my stomach. It was easy to disappear into the fields—my body seemed to blend in like I was just a part of the land. After months at the farm, my skin was tan. There were lines around my eyes and on my forehead. My fingernails held crescents of dark soil. My knees and elbows, although scrubbed, were dirty.

That weekend I planned to drive up to Cabot, Vermont to attend my mother's family reunion. Every first Sunday of August for the past forty years they had gathered on the lawn of their dairy farm at the top of a long dirt road where, from the clustered picnic tables, we could look out to the purple folds of the Green Mountains. I'd never felt more connected to that side of my family than I did that morning after Jayden's disappearance, when I felt called in some way back to the land. I looked forward to appearing at the family reunion in this new skin, this body of a farm girl. I wore my sweat-stained baseball cap, just as I remembered the old uncles wore, the brim's lip lined with salt. My blue jean shorts were slick, almost oily with wear. The toes of my boots shined, not from polish but from work.

As I unfolded out of the car with my siblings, I hoped that I would be welcomed. My brother and sisters and I were always distinctly different from the other children and young people gathered there. Although only an hour's drive separated us the contrast between our college town the their rural home was striking. Maybe they wouldn't look at me so strangely or for so long if I told them about the farm I worked on. I couldn't wait to respond to their question of "What do you do?" with, "I'm a farmer." On that old hill, surrounded by the bones of my ancestors tucked into the cemetery near the heifers' pasture, I'd feel like I belonged.

Year after year my mother's family gathered and posed for a picture under the same old sugar maple. There was a wall in the old farm house where copies of these images stretched back into black and white. As kids, we'd scatter as soon as the photo was taken, the burst of flash releasing us. We'd run out across the road to the family graveyard, or into the barn to feed the calves or search the hayloft for nests of newborn kittens, or out into the sugar bush to hunt wild blackberries. Only after a long while, or at the call of my mother's voice, would the four of us return to sit dutifully at the picnic tables, resting our elbows on the sticky checkered tablecloth.

Always, some great-uncle with deep-set eyes and weather-beaten skin manned a series of grills on the farmhouse porch, flipping frozen burger patties and hot dogs under a thunderhead of smoke. A great-aunt, bent as a dried sunflower stalk, brought a cooler full of lobsters from her home in Maine. Another great-uncle tended a huge pot of boiling water set above a wood fire where the lobsters were dipped and cooked until they were red as strawberries. In the garage bay, where tractors and milk trucks were repaired, the aunts and female cousins set up folding tables. Talking quietly to each other they stacked up side dishes and desserts: quivering Jell-O molds, cherry pies, chocolate cupcakes, macaroni, and potato salad thick with mayonnaise. My brother and sisters and I scooped up and served ourselves huge plates of food and then, sitting beneath the shade of the sugar maple, snapped open the shells of our lobsters and dipped them into cups of clarified butter. For a few minutes, we'd allow the aunts and uncles to meet us as if for the first time, to pinch cheeks or tousle hair, before dumping our plates into the garbage bins and fleeing again to the huge, sprawling farmyard.

But for the first time in decades, it was raining up on the hill during the reunion. Heavy clouds veiled the long view out into the mountains. Our family picture was taken under the eaves of the porch instead of beneath the sugar maple's shade. I'd never seen a photograph on the old wallpapered hall where the family was posed under the eaves. We packed in tightly for the shot, while the rain rang on the metal roofing. Shoulder to shoulder, the short great uncles leaning, the heavyset aunts poking forward, aprons first. Then quickly we all broke apart. The old uncles went to the grills and lobster pot, lighting cigars and cigarettes under the brims of their caps. The aunts tightened their apron strings and filtered back into the garage to prepare the picnic sides.

I stood under the porch roof as the rain curtained the mountain view and wondered where I should go.

My siblings had escaped into the dim, musty farmhouse to sit on hard chairs around the dining table. My mother and father gathered in the kitchen, helping the oldest aunt clarify butter. Because of the rain, the garage bays had been cleared out and the picnic tables which usually lined the yard were carried inside. Water dripped off the roof and flooded the oily concrete floor. Under the flickering fluorescent work lights, my aunts and female cousins served up their salads, mixing in mayo and mustard, slicing their pies into huge triangles. The men who weren't tending the grills or fire sat along one long end of a picnic table, talking about the weather. Their eyes were hidden under the lamplights. They spoke in the thick accent of northern Vermont, quick barks, followed by drawn-out interior vowels. I couldn't tell if they noticed me. I grabbed a soda from the coolers, snapped open the mouth and sat down alone to watch the rain.

When the lobsters were reddened and cooling on their tray the garage filled with bodies. The smell of cows. Sweet hay. Raw milk. Cigars. WD-40. Off-road diesel. Butter. Grill smoke. Beer. Wet leather. My brother and sisters slipped in beside me on the picnic table bench with loaded plates and sweating cans of soda. They rolled their eyes and looked longingly at our car parked on the side of the dirt road.

My mother sat near and began, as she always did, to introduce us again to her relatives. I clutched my hands together until they were pink, waiting for her to get to me and tell them all that I was a farmer. When she finally mentioned that I worked at a farm the men answered my mother's statement with a simple *yuup*. One old uncle asked how tall our corn was. I told him we'd already been harvesting it for a month, realizing too late that he meant feed corn instead of the sweet corn we were growing. He nodded and went back to crushing the shell of his lobster. I knew suddenly that they saw me not as an insider but as an impostor. Because I tended vegetables. Because I grew organically and mostly, although they'd never say it, because I was a woman. My face flushed and I pulled my hat brim low.

Quickly my brother and sisters and I emptied our plates and slipped them into the trash. After dessert and a few forced hugs, we zipped up our raincoats and rushed back to the car. The tires kicked up mud as we turned around and made our way back down the hill, past the graveyard where my grandmother and grandfather lay under their shared headstone. Wet dairy cows stood quietly behind the wooden fence.

On the drive south, along the bumpy roads, my brother and sisters fell asleep, resting their heads against each other and the windows. I looked out at the road, at the rain-washed farmhouses and decaying barns, at hayfields and flower gardens, yards both tidy and cluttered.

"I don't think I'm the sort of farmer they're used to." I said to no one in particular.

My mother asked me about my college classes and I knew that what she was really saying was *stay in school*. She didn't want me to be a farmer; after all, she'd chosen to move off that hill. I listed my courses off to her flatly. What was I? I wondered. I stood somewhere between two identities, the girl in pearls whom my mother was proud of—the girl who was going back to college, back to the boy she'd once loved, and this other girl, this dirty farm girl, dressed as I was dressed in the car, in clothing that smelled like sweat and soil. I tried to push the thought of leaving to the very edge of my consciousness. If I even brushed against the idea my heart sunk, waterlogged. There was no room to move, to work, to breathe, with a heart like that. But I knew, just as I knew that the days were getting shorter, that the grasses were yellowing, that the melons were ripening and the winter squash beginning to sweat sugar through their skin, that I'd have to go. Driving home, we passed geese, picking feed out of a cut hayfield and I thought of their winged migration, down mountains and river guideways, and wondered if that move hurt or if it was something lighter in their breasts, something sweet.

On Saturday mornings it is my job to leave the farm and set up a booth at the farmers market in a town downriver. The market starts the last weekend in May just as the world is opening to green and heat. It is a task that I've earned, like seeding and harvesting asparagus, and I feel proud to be asked to perform it. I enjoy being the face of the crew, the only one of us who gets to share what they grow directly with a customer. I am the farmer in their eyes. It surprises people to see a young woman in this role and if they doubt me, I draw them back in with my stories. I can smile all day and describe our products like a seed catalog. Words are something I cultivate like plants. They roll and grow as lush as squash vines on my tongue. It's my stories, as well as the displays of vegetables, that make people stay and shop. I learn these secrets like I learn how to start a seed or pick a berry. I've been going to market for the farm for the past few summers and I know that the best sales are early in the year, when everyone in town grows excited to be outside again, eating fresh pastries out of brown bags and filling wicker baskets with bright pink radishes and bunches of thin, local asparagus. It's a commerce of hope.

The market ground sits on a flat yard between a local hardware store and a hayfield which in early spring is just beginning to flush with green. Between the store and the yard, young apple trees drop blankets of pink petals under their shaded skirts. The hayfield across the road is small and neatly mowed. It comes to an end up against a bank of white pine and maples as the land climbs into gentle hills. Between cuttings, the farmer parks his blue and white New Holland tractor at the edge of the grass and it casts shadows like a sundial. When business is slow or the day drags cold and rainy, I stare out at the field and imagine myself in the grass, on my hands and knees, weeding.

I must have the tent set up before the opening bell at 8:00 A.M., so Saturdays start early, even earlier than other farm mornings. I bike to Cedar Circle before there is much light in the sky. Not even Itchi the cat is awake; he's still curled in some secret place beneath the barn. The fields lie still like they, too, are sleeping. Night's odd colorlessness rests strange upon the plants. They grow and breathe without us tending them, in those long intervals of darkness. I feel almost out of place, walking across the road to the shop. Maybe I'm waking them too early? I tiptoe but there is no way to start the key without making a sound. I roar the big market van to life, its diesel engine shaking the stillness from the dawn. Carefully, I back it up to the double barn doors and with the help of Robert, who comes up from the staff parking lot still lacing on his boots, we load crates of vegetables onto the van's shelves. Coins rattle in the metal cash box as I carry it across the driveway. The market is an exchange where the weight of our soil and water and toil and sweat comes back locked in the hard metal cash box. But the idea doesn't cheapen the day —there are bellies to feed, beautiful dinners to be hosted. All the ingredients of these meals are packed and washed and stacked high in the back of the market van.

Robert and I fill water bottles and make ourselves tea in the café, the steam flushing our cheeks in the bite of dawn. We pull the van behind the greenhouses and grab the flowers I set aside the day before. The tea steeps darkly in our mugs as Robert hangs the baskets on brackets above the crates of vegetables and I line the flats of plants on the shelves welded to the body of the van. We settle into our seats and reach for our cups, taking a look behind my shoulder at the locked stacks of crates and the swaying hanging flower baskets, bright even in morning's dim light. Before turning onto the main road, I run one last check over the list of market essentials in my head and quickly tally up how much money we can make if we sell all of our cargo. Soon, I'll be pressing what I've grown into the palms of customers, handing off the fruits of our labor.

Downriver the sun rises gently, the fog spreads pink to golden at the eastern edge of the hills and the water reflects sky and field between serpentine banks. Halfway to the market, the river bends as the road climbs and across the waters, in New Hampshire, Dartmouth's stand of ancient white pines lifts in a solid, vertical wall of green. Dawn casts clean shadows off the trees like the sun through a canyon. In the back of the van, the crates rock and creak, hanging baskets sway, dusting the flowers with a neon confetti of petals. My prayers on a market morning are for empty crates, thick stacks of bills in the cash box, and big crowds, their hands dancing over the displays hungrily.

Robert and I sell asparagus, spinach, radishes, Swiss chard, arugula, lettuce, scallions, salad mix, bok choy, flowers, and hanging baskets. The vegetables are young and tender, still softly spring-like. I handle them delicately because they will easily bruise or wilt. When we arrive, passing the van through an aisle of apple trees, I first cast out the tablecloths and smooth them over the tables, then stack our wooden display shelves. Robert carries over the crates of produce while I arrange each crop and hook a handwritten price sign beside it. We loop hanging baskets on the metal frame of the tent and set flats of vegetable starts and flowers out like small gardens, growing from the shade of our canopy onto the market ground's fresh wood-mulched aisle.

When the display is complete, I step back into the walkway to look at it, ambling by like a customer might. I duck in to rotate a bunch of radishes and straighten a price tag, getting everything just right, settled in the perfect place between order and casual messiness. Too nice and people will take pictures but not buy anything. Too sloppy and they won't stop to look. By the time the manager rings his brass bell declaring the market open for business Robert and I stand behind the tables, with Cedar Circle aprons and baseball caps on, sipping our tea and splitting off soft flakes of fresh croissants from the vendor across the lawn.

At lunch we slip away, one at a time, to purchase food from the other tents. I always buy an orzo salad made with chopped herbs and local goat cheese from a Greek family. Robert buys meat pies from a British baker and glass quarts of raw milk from a couple of old sisters who work a dairy farm along the river. The milk is oyster-white and thick. He has to shake the glass to break up the ring of cream in its throat. While one of us sits on the red cooler eating our market lunch in the shade of the tent the other stands and works. I watch the back of Robert's legs and his hands gesturing as he describes the peppery bite of arugula or the wet crunch of spring radishes. The sun rises and rotates over our shoulders. I plant my feet firmly on the market lawn, my boots gripping the wet grass and wood chips, my hands resting on the hips of my blue jeans, watching, with pride, as our display shrinks, vegetable by vegetable, bunch by bunch until there is more tablecloth and apple crate showing than greenery. Here the circle completes itself. What we grow leaves us.

CHAPTER SEVEN

My days following Jayden's departure in late August were long and heavy with sweat. After biking home I often collapsed in a heat stroke nap and would wake, dry-mouthed, to a late dinner, my head empty and heavy. In my bedroom, I opened my laptop and looked for Jayden's messages as I'd once checked the mail for his handwritten letters during the first year of our love. I had a box of those envelopes in my closet, a stacked inventory of our romance, a history of promises. But now his emails arrived with no pattern or grace. In reply I wrote about rent, utilities, how high to set the thermostat in the Portland apartment. The solid one, the planner. This also meant that I could easily become the boring one and I felt stung to think of how he might read my practical messages while drunk or stoned, reciting poetry to the summer lights over the city. Here I was, this tired girl with an aching back and dirty hands worried about how much electricity he was using and where to slip the rent check in the manager's office. But at least I had something to say. At least I had some way to be part of us.

Jayden wrote to me, first from California, and then from our apartment in Portland. He'd arrived early, he said, to set up the space. His words were either short statements or long intoxicated love poems. Nothing in between. He spoke of the dust on our countertops, how he thought of me when he saw our books, our wine glasses, my heels by the closet door, empty. In California, there was pain and its cure. Bottles of it, he wrote, made for horses but just as good for his back. At night in Oregon it was still hot and he'd go downtown without me and wander the halls of Powell's Books, searching for some second-hand copy, or flipping through heavy coffee table volumes of photography. He was, I felt, living some sort of a ghost version of our life and I wondered if I was there with him in spirit. I didn't feel anything different, no sense of being split in two ways.

I painted the back room; he wrote to me. *I moved my things in there.* Our back room in Portland was a guest bedroom where we stored our clothing and kept an air mattress for friends. Our cat liked to sit in its windows and watch people pass along the walkway outside. Light came late to that room and only lasted for a few hours so that it was always damp and moldy. But now it was Jayden's and the apartment wasn't ours as it had been.

The physical division of our lives broke what was left of my heart. I had once loved the mingling of our belongings. Our clothing tossed together in the laundry. Our cups spilling into each other in the sink. Our books and records shuffled on the shelf. We hadn't worried about ownership, only about surrounding ourselves with what we found beautiful and essential. Who owned the record player? I wondered. And which records were mine and which were his? How could I give four years of myself away in things, dividing the harvest of our time between two lives? The screen of my laptop lit my face at night in my bedroom as I tried to type out a reply. How to respond to such a split, cut like a storm-broken tree right down the middle? Heat lightning flickered above the field outside my window. My hands were worn and smelled like garlic. I'd been cleaning bulbs all day and garlic oil had worked its way into every pore and cut, stinging and sweet.

$$\maltese$$

August smells like garlic, a harvest that signals a goodbye to summer. It is a smell that I both dread and adore. It gets in my skin and seeps into my blood. I chew it raw between my molars as a cure for colds and even heartbreak. My hands grow dry from touching it and my fingerprints begin to peel back as if my identity is being gradually erased. In the garlic, in the white, hot cloves, the history of the farm is contained and tending to it I tell myself its story. Time is a wheel and all that grows comes by revolution.

Garlic has its own calendar, a cycle off track from every other crop. It is unique among all the plants we tend, like an unexpected visitor. It goes into the ground in late October, when there is still a little warmth in the sun but the nights chill the soil solid. Each clove is a seed so to plant garlic first we break up the bulb like chefs into tapered, papery cloves. In November we spread straw mulch over the garlic and through the winter it sleeps dormant in the frozen ground. Something in its heart needs those days of darkness and cold.

Garlic breaks through the mulch soon after snowmelt, the first green flag that the farm is alive. In early summer the crew snaps off the swirling loops of scapes from the garlic plants. The scapes, if left untended, will flower purple and develop tiny seedpods, sapping the plant's energy, drawing it up away from the bulb. As the days grow longer and hotter, we watch the leaves, one by one, fall dead and golden, clinging crisply to the hard stalk. They begin to drop in mid-July, the first signs of the summer's end. Luke counts up from the bulb until seven of the nine garlic leaves are dried and brown. During a window of dry weather, a sliver of high pressure between August storms, we pull the garlic and hang it to dry. By the end of the month, as the first crew members leave for school, those who remain begin cleaning and sorting it, saving seed for next year and selling the rest.

All things start small, I tell myself as I clean the garlic. The first year we planted garlic Luke bought in the seed stuffed in a brown paper bag from the organic grocery store. I wasn't at the farm when that first garlic was planted—I was in boarding school in Michigan. I imagine that Luke and Justin planted the first crop together, one dark October day. I think of them consulting their library of farming books, flipping through agricultural journals at the start of the row, deciding together, after much debate, to plant each clove six inches or twelve inches apart, and how deep to press them. Luke I imagine drawing out numbers and figures in one of his notebooks with his carpenter's pencil, and Justin planning far out into the future, asking big questions about problems that haven't surfaced yet but wanting to work through them in advance.

I was away at school through that fall and winter, as the first garlic slowly took root in the cold soil. I didn't see the garlic shoots break the straw mulch, bright green spears after a week of sunny weather in April. When I came back to work on the crew the garlic was already knee-high and thick-leaved, a sword of a plant. That first row was bunched and hung to dry in the barn. The bulbs were small and grey and it took me a long afternoon in the processing area to clean them up to white, peeling away the dirty layers of outer skin until they glowed like moonlight. That first harvest we mostly saved for seed, only the tiniest bulbs went off to the kitchen to flavor pesto or mole.

Garlic is an investment, collecting interest, growing bigger over time. It's a long-term relationship, built on hope. Through careful sorting and deliberate saving, the crop improves, each summer bigger than the last until the bulbs are the size of golf balls, then the size of tight fists. It isn't just the process of sorting and saving for the best traits, keeping desired genetics on the farm, but the plants themselves that begin to change and adapt. Garlic is a chameleon, shifting to acclimate the conditions in which it grows, the acidity of the soil, the humidity of the air, day length, temperature, the flavor of rainwater. It changes in the land like we do. I read that after seven full seasons of seed savings and growing out, garlic becomes a specific variety of the place it has grown. It becomes the land. It is ours and we are in it too.

Each fall we plant a little more, sometimes buying additional seed from a farmer further up the valley, a man who is only ever referred to as Boots. Boots brings us his largest bulb to brag every year, until one fall we show him our biggest garlic and he says he won't sell to us anymore. But by that point, we don't need any more seed.

Because of its cycle, its own internal clock, garlic is touched by the crew in every season. It's planted in the fall by those that remain when everyone else has flown back to school. The scapes are snapped off in the early summer right when students return, flushing the fields with their loud conversation. Then in August the crew pulls the plants, hangs them to dry and a few weeks later begins cleaning and sorting the cloves until again it is fall and the seed garlic returns to the soil. For years the garlic grows like this, on a great wheel, again and again so that everyone who ever worked on the field crew touches the crop at some point in its cycle. All their hands are in it, under its skin, in its flesh.

We pull the garlic plants on a dry day in the afternoon. During a rainstorm the week before, I cut and tie slings to loop around the plants, using my arms as a guide for length. Everyone on the crew hangs the ropes I knotted around their arms or slings them across their chest like bandoliers. The garlic plants are crisp and the straw around them sizzles old and brown. I pull up each plant carefully and tap it against my shin, knocking off a bit of dirt from the root ball. I welcome each scratch and insect bite. They draw me back to the fields.

When I've collected a bunch of ten garlic plants, I loop the string around the necks and pull it closed. A long piece of string hangs above the leaves so it can be tied to the trellis strung from the rafters of the barn. I slip each bunch into an orange harvesting basket and when it's full, I carry it to the end of the row and load it into Yoda. Back in the field, sweat rolls down my legs. My arms are red and stinging. I am just movement, heat, sweat, garlic oil. As soon as the truck bed is full, I hop into the passenger seat and ride up to the barn with Luke, enjoying, for a few minutes, the breeze on our forearms and music breaking the hot silence of the afternoon. We park outside the big red barn and haul the baskets upstairs. They aren't heavy but the garlic leaves are dry and scratch our arms. The center stems where the scapes have been snapped cut like whips. We lay the bunches out on the floor and then carefully loop the strings over tight lines of ropes, using a number four-shaped knot that hangs tight but can be pulled down with a simple slip.

Out in the field, the rows where the garlic grew are stripped bare in an afternoon. Only the weeds remain, scattered and weak, dropping where they lost the trellis of the garlic's bold spears. Like a person with all their supports removed, I think. The emptied row makes me feel hopeless. But in the barn, sitting under the bunches of garlic hanging from the rafters I imagine being underground, in the soil, looking up at their roots and higher still, the sky, and I fill with joy at the weight above me, a physical representation of so much faith. Up there the dust smells like garlic. Luke and I set the box fans blowing on the root balls and the whole barn stirs with the whirling smell of drying garlic.

I take home a few of the raw bulbs that had slipped out of the strings. The skins aren't dry so they are hard to peel and the flesh is almost too spicy, fresh and biting. I scratch them along toasted bread from the farmers market for a quick dinner after work. Garlic burns my lips. My sheets smell like garlic. Those garlic nights anchor me to the farm, story becoming memory as the sun sets.

As I clean garlic, I imagine all the people who touched it before and are now gone. Justin, who planted the very first crop, is now in law school. I know that ghosts don't go far, they settle into the cloves and when I touch the garlic, I remember them. I draw out those summers from all the other seasons and feel them again—Justin's laugh, and Sarah's big smile. The garlic is better because of them, improved by all the people who handled it. Like the ghosts in the barn that linger, brushing their old tools, called into life by sweat and routines, the garlic collects a history of work. We work. We grow. The garlic swells with that pattern. It multiplies and draws out into elegant, teardrop bulbs with tapered necks and skin as thin as rolling paper, tough enough to survive a Vermont winter, and so sweet that it caramelizes when roasted into deep, brown, garlic sugar. I think of my future like that, improving each year until my doubts fade into sheets of white promise.

So much of what I do at the farm can be weighed and measured. The garlic is the slowest and most deliberate success, from a few pounds of seed in a brown paper bag to thousands of pounds of the farm's own plants, strung up, like constellations across the dark, tar paper roof the barn. Garlic gives me hope that I am part of something essential.

CHAPTER EIGHT

August was a month of goodbyes, the earliest birds leaving for warmer climates. It wasn't just me making the migration away from the fields. The whole crew divided, our gang breaking into smaller and smaller bands as the month faded in September. In the last week of my time at the farm, I grew softer and let the loss hit me hard like a fist in the stomach. I doubled over to it. Everything was bittersweet. Hot days when I blinked back sweat and blacked out from exhaustion became romantic and I would pause and try to remember that feeling of fading. Mornings were particularly beautiful, fresh and lush, the fullest part of the year before death and frost withered the vines. I looked at my friends differently too; they became even more beloved. They were my family. My brothers and sisters. Soon, I wouldn't be part of their story. Soon, I'd be a ghost too, like all the others in the garlic.

When we stood together near the truck in the morning—smoking and planning the day—I watched us, this circle of misfits, and knew that I had found a home. These were my people, with dirty hands and canvas shorts slick from wear and wash. Young men with sunburnt necks and a week's worth of stubble. Women in loose shirts or bikini tops, strong through the leg and shoulder, leaning up against the side of Yoda. The sadness made me love harder. Some days it was almost impossible not to cry. I wore dark glasses and my tears and sweat mixed into saltwater on my face. I biked home weeping, feeling that by leaving this place I was abandoning someone who needed me.

But always there was Jayden, right behind the farm. Jayden, who, like a plant, I wondered if I could nurse back to health. Maybe I was leaving one thing that needed me for another whose need was just as powerful. Saying goodbye to the fields filled me with a sense of sadness as dark as a rainy night, damp and heavy. The sorrow drowned me and lay over the top of my heartbreak. As the weeks passed, one brilliant, hot, exhausting day after another, I grew increasingly depressed. I was terrified of returning to Portland, of being back in that familiar but utterly altered space with a boy who I'd once known but who was now, in many ways, a stranger. I wanted to be in a place where I knew myself. That place, I realized just as I was leaving it, was the farm. But there were classes, flights, and tuition all nailing me to different futures.

"You'll do well in school," my mother would say to me at dinner, "you always do." The girl in pearls was top of her class. She had medals from the President. She had awards. She was good at doing what everyone expected of her. She excelled at shape-shifting. As I packed my bags, folding my school clothes, I wondered if I'd be able to make that change, from farm girl to college student. Maybe, I thought, I'd break down like Jayden had broken in Paris. But I couldn't afford that kind of split. I didn't, either as the girl in pearl earrings or as a farm girl, shatter so easily. I zipped up my bags and dragged them downstairs. I felt my life moving forward like a spring flood and all I could do was stay afloat.

Jayden messaged me to ask what time my flight was coming in. He was looking forward to seeing me, he said. He'd pick me up. I imagined him waiting for me outside the terminal, and how once upon a time my heart would have beat faster to think of him there–his curls, his dark sunglasses, his soft hands on the wheel–but now I only grew heavy. The work ahead of me seemed impossible. It was up to me to heal us and grow something out of the ruins of our summer. But I was already heartbroken.

On my last night at the farm sparks shot up into the stars as we set a stack of logs ablaze. Fires were the crew's way of saying farewell but that night we were also celebrating what had been our best growing year on record. Kate, one of the farm's owners, swept in wearing a long colorful skirt and passed around handwritten accounting numbers. We flipped through them, proud and disbelieving. *Convert that money into pounds, into crates of tomatoes or flats of strawberries, pints of blueberries, bushels of corn, boxes of watermelons, bunches of beets, parsley or spinach,* we whispered. Nick, Luke and I sat around a wicker table on the porch of the cabin, saying goodbye without saying much at all. The paper rested near a flickering citronella candle.

First, we toasted ourselves. Then, deeper in the night, we grew quiet. Between inhalations, we watched smoke rise up to the roofline. We were past expressing complexities but the silence was fear, the fear of the next step. We knew we could do more, be better, work harder. We had proved ourselves through all those years of weeding, of small yields, of slow learning. They had paid off, but there was still so much to improve. We sat with the weight of that.

Around the table, as the sunset drifted into dark and the fire snapped down to hard black coals, we formed the idea that the land thrived off our blood, sweat, and tears. To make it better we simply had to bleed, sweat, and cry more—we had to wring ourselves out for those acres. At twenty-one my body was becoming stiff, my wrists singing with nerve damage, my fingers numbed, my back twisted. We sat there, gathering the courage for another year just as I was gathering the strength to return to college and to Jayden.

It was late. Past the hour to drive home. Past the hour to get enough sleep to be rested. I tended the fire by the river, knocking logs into the center. Nick and Luke were drunk and hardly able to move from their chairs. I watched their cigarettes flare in the darkness. The beer had settled in my stomach and I felt that deep sadness of being no longer drunk. All I wanted was to sleep. Behind the trunk of one of the big spruce trees that framed the dock, I pulled off my clothing and untied my shoes. Our fire cast a little dying light onto the water. There was no moon and the sky was full of stars. I walked down the center of the dock, my skin tingling, delighting in being naked in the night air.

It was warm still, even though high in the hills the maples and birches were turning to red and yellow. I sat with my feet dangling then pushed myself under. My toes brushed water grass and the soft silt of the riverbed. I swam quietly out to the middle of the river, where the stars lay on the smooth surface. I made them ripple with my strokes. With my ears at the water's lips I could hear the fire falling in on itself, crunching and crackling. My friends' voices slurred and deep, the sound of glass on glass as they set their beers down. The river lapped softly along the shore. I flipped onto my back and floated face up, swimming in between stars, tiny and beautiful and completely alone in the breath of darkness.

I flew back to Portland early on a clear day. As we neared landing, the missing shoulder of Mount St. Helens appeared out my window. *Violence*, it said. *Power*. A world reformed. The volcano erupted five years before I was born and still, the landscape was a raw wound. If I looked closer from my tiny airplane window, I saw trees re-growing, water running clear through banks of naked, exploded trees that were slowly turning to rotten driftwood, ragged as old ghosts.

Jayden and I had hiked near the slopes of that volcano, up an easy trail to June Lake where we'd posed ourselves for a photo which another hiker took for us on our disposable camera. On that afternoon I tucked myself into his shoulder and he hovered above me, his curls casting long shadows in my hair. I remember the feeling of that mountain near us, potent and living, almost beating like a heart beneath our feet. How the winding roads had sickened my stomach up and down from the park. Jayden had taken them fast, while I'd clutched the handrail and held my breath. The day had been electric with fear and fresh air.

Flying into Portland I was terrified of even the smallest eruption. As I waited for my luggage, I plotted my return to the apartment, how I'd touch Jayden's arm, not his hand in the car, how I'd lock the bathroom door while showering and wear pajamas to bed. It wasn't our place anymore. Maybe, I thought, we could make it work in this new format, we could grow with our love flattened and charred. My cat grumbled in her box and I reached through the mesh siding to stroke her ears. Where would she sleep at night, I wondered? In my bed or Jayden's?

Outside the air was humid and fragrant with the last of landscaping's flowers. I sat on a bench and watched cars drift in and out, picking up passengers then slipping away out onto the interstate. Jayden was late. Night came to the spruces and turned them blue. I imagined neon lights snapping and flickering as they came on downtown. When Jayden's car pulled around the corner it was speeding and slammed to a stop. His hair, I saw through the windshield, was a mess, and as he got out to help me load my bags, he was barefoot and his sweatpants were slick and unwashed. He smelled stronger than ripe; something had gone sour on his body. I knew he was stoned.

Before I could raise my arms, he hugged and squeezed my shoulders hard, lifting me off the ground. He was smiling when I looked up at him, flushed and dazed like a messy sunset.

"Good to have you back," he said to me, and then he lifted the cat carrier and kissed the cat's face through the black mesh.

In the car he was all energy, poetry, music. "Listen to this line from The Doors, here check out this bootleg Dylan, I've been reading Dylan Thomas, reciting him, and Neruda in Spanish? Just for the sound."

He changed CDs, he did his Dylan Thomas imper-sonation, bare feet on the pedals, fingers white on the stick. I shrank in my seat, reduced, immediately, to the girl at his side. The farm fell away behind us and my arms felt light and weak. There was no going back. Tomorrow I'd have to go shopping for school supplies. I'd have to hang up my clothing and buy books at the college. I'd put on pearl earrings and patent leather flats and blow dry my hair to shining. And I'd wake up in an apartment split in two.

We stopped at the grocery store at the foot of the hill near our apartment and I bought two bottles of red wine. Jayden told me that self-medication was his mantra now, the easiest way to fix any problem. I bought flowers too, clipped and trim in a sheet of plastic cellophane. Their faces looked at me bright and blank as I held the bouquet in my lap, the necks of the two wine bottles clinking in their paper bag. During the summer I drank after work, at parties, never alone. But that night wine seemed like the best way out of my skin.

Jayden carried the cat, the wine, and the bouquet up the three flights of slippery wooden stairs to our apartment while I dragged my heavy bag, folding over under the weight of a backpack stuffed with books. The air smelled piney and damp. Nothing had changed, except for us. Inside, I set my bags by the door and went immediately to the kitchen for a glass of wine. Dirty dishes were piled in the sink. Pill bottles marched in rows of yellow and orange, white-capped, along the breakfast bar. In the recycling bin empty bottles of wine, whiskey, and gin glittered. But the walls were still the same electric salmon and outside I could see the lights of the city encircled by the dark shapes of mountains. I grabbed a coffee cup because all the wine glasses were dirty and poured it full to the brim, its dark tannic breath opening under my lips, rich as soil.

I drank like I was thirsty. My face flushed. My heart settled. I was sleepy, suddenly, in a sweet, dreamy way.

"Let me show you my room," Jayden said, leading me down the hallway. The smell of the place hit me first. Rank and feral. The trash was piled with takeout containers. The air hung heavy with whiskey and tobacco. He'd painted the walls a dark green, fading to black in the shadows so that all the light seemed to cling to the ceiling fixture. In the corner the air mattress sagged, stacked with books and records. Against the windows, he'd set up a desk made from a board laid over cinder blocks. There, his typewriter rested like some quiet beast, surrounded by a field of crumbled paper. On one wall he'd hung a poster of two girls in bed, kissing. I didn't say anything. I didn't understand any of it. The color, the poster, the smell. I thought I knew Jayden—we'd grown up together—but all of this had come from a place in him that I'd never seen. I looked at him like he was a stranger, in the dim light, with his head haloed by auburn curls. He stood, slouched like an elderly man, bent through the back. His eyes were hot with what? With pain?

I let the cat loose to stalk the apartment. In the kitchen I sank the store-bought flowers into a vase. Jayden slid open the door to the porch. There the air dropped dead three stories below to the street and the city spread itself in a quilt of lights out to the lap of the mountains. We set our mugs on the glass table and lit up cigarettes, burning through one after the other as the wine softened and melted away everything that was hurting. There was nothing to say. In the light of his smokes, Jayden looked older to me and I didn't want to touch him. I couldn't think of kissing him. Instead, I felt the need to care for him.

He was worse than I'd thought; the pain twisted him. It filled up all the places in him that had once been radiant with light and words. I licked the last grains of wine from the rim of my mug and wondered if I could save him; if, with things as simple as sun and water, a person could grow like a sick plant, from something thin and yellow to something thick and green. This would be my last act as his lover, I thought, blazing my mind up briefly with nicotine. I'd nurse him back to health.

Late into the night, we stumbled back inside and he tripped down the white strip of carpet to the back room. I watched his lurch, his back hunched and strange to me. The room was spinning so I lay down alone on the huge bed in the living room and stared up at the poked ceiling. A new day was rising in the fields along the river in Vermont. I could feel the light changing, the humidity raising up sheets of spun fog from the surface of the river. But I fought and pulled myself back into my body, feeling heavy, numb. The edges of the room blurred to black and the cat settled on the pillow, flicking me with her tail. The noises of the apartment complex started in around the din ringing in my ears. Water pipes rushing. People tripping around their carpets. Televisions murmuring. Sirens screaming, dogs howling in the hills. Outside cars slipped by like water over rocks. The rush of the interstate, the rush of the rivers. City sounds. I was alone in them. I hugged a pillow to my chest and fell asleep drifting above the sheets, in a room which was strange to me.

☙

I drive down the dusty central road to the river with the setting sun already casting long shadows in the rows. The kale plants reach long towards the east. I set a tent up near the weedy corner of the bottom field, where the land slips into the river. It's an oddly rounded overgrown lot where we bury farm animals when they die. Chickens and cats, mostly, sleep beneath that patch of soil, but there's also the pigeon with broken wings Sarah tried to heal and bones older than our memories churned up in the plow blade each spring. I tell my parents I am sleeping over with a girlfriend but in truth I have no friends save for the ones here, at the farm, that I plan on spending the night with. Inside the tent, the world is just light and sounds and I lay there for a minute, wondering if Will and Kate will let me pitch it there for the rest of the summer. I think of how nice it would be to hear morning come to the fields as the birds sang the sun up and how much more work I would get done sleeping there at the edge of the river and not having to pedal back and forth from home each day.

After rolling out my sleeping bag I walk up along the southern edge of the road where the trees cast the dirt in shadow all day. The earth is cool on my bare feet. Around me the afternoon shadows are stretching towards the river, dragging the shape of the tomato trellis into a solid wall. On the lawn around the farm stand the crews gather, not just the field crew with their deep tans, their hands and knees still dirty after scrubbing, but the farm stand and greenhouse staff, as well as the bookkeeper and the woman who works in the kitchen alchemizing our bolted basil into creamy pesto, our mountains of tomatoes into salsa. Everyone is dressed better than they are at work. Grinning, they drift in, carrying trays of food and heavy cases of beer. Smoke clouds from the grill by The Yellow House and citronella candles keep post around the yard's perimeter, burning sweet and sharp. The only other person at the party younger than me is Cyrus and he shows me his water bottle when I set my kebabs down on the picnic table. Turning his back to the crew he unscrews the cap and holds it under my nose.

"It's vodka," he whispers, his green eyes shining.

As the others mingle around the grills and the tables,

Cyrus and I nurse the bottle, wandering around the edges of the farm until night falls and everyone is drunk. When it's empty we come up from the fields and sit on the lawn in the bright squares of light falling from The Yellow House's windows. The crew clusters in groups, passing pipes and cigarettes. Smoke hangs above in the low branches of the maple tree.

I swipe a fistful of cold bottles, brown necked and sweating and, handing one to Cyrus, we step away from the patches of light. With the low murmur of late night conversation behind us we sit on the side of the road, with our legs out on the warm cement, trying to flick open the bottles with the side of a lighter. My knuckles shave along the edge of the cap.

"Fuck." I try again, wedging it harder, and the cap springs open. I hand the bottle to Cyrus and open one for myself. It's cold and delicious and nice to hold the chilled glass in my hands which are somehow still warm and stiff from the day. The beer sweats against my thighs when I put it down. I light a cigarette and Cyrus fumbles in his pocket and lights one too. The nicotine makes my brain buzz and my heart speed up.

"Come on," Cyrus says, crawling into the center of the road. "Come on."

I grab my beer and inch forward until we are lying in the middle of the road with our arms and legs spread like starfish, our beers set off to one side. Looking up at the stars we drag our burning cigarettes through the night sky like we are trying to connect the constellations with those sparks. The road is warm and flat on my back but pressed above me I can feel the vast chill of the heavens, pouring down from the Milky Way.

When a car passes on the state highway, across the cornfield to the west, I think I can hear it rumbling through the earth. Pavillion Road runs flat and straight on either end of us and all the houses along the way are dark and silent. We would see any oncoming traffic long before it reached us. But fear is electric and shakes every part of my body awake. Smoke in my lungs, booze in my belly, and my limbs shaking with what might happen. My skin is a little warm on one side from the road and cool on the other from the huge night sky.

As soon as the fear burns off, we stand up and sway. The party has gone somewhere else it seems and the lawn is black, the eyes of The Yellow House windows seem closed. Cyrus stumbles over to the garage by the big greenhouse. He grabs a red plastic can and pours gasoline on the road. I jump at the smell and reach for his arm. "Come on, quit it." He pushes me out of the way and then touches the flame of his lighter to the ground. The gas catches fire in one big rush, making a sound like all the air leaving someone's lungs. On the cement the flames are blue and above it, they turn yellow and orange. I can make out black smoke drifting higher. The fire is in the shape of a number eight which Cyrus has shakily poured out of the gas can in big sweeps and arches. It is bright enough for a second that I can see the hedgerow and the cornfields and just make out the shape of the hills to the east. Then the eight fades and goes dark. Something inside of me shifts and I am suddenly very tired and sad.

Cyrus reaches for the gas can again but I shake my head. "Nah, I'm over it."

The stars are bright and far away and I am scared of something I can't name. I say goodnight to Cyrus and walk back along the dark road, down the length of the home farm. My feet know the path but the dirt is cold now and I wrap my arms around my shoulders.

That night I sleep like I am drowning under ice and wake up early to the birds screaming. I drive home and change and come back to the farm for work, my head heavy and my throat dry. We load up Yoda and drive down the road to the blueberry patch. I sit on the tailgate with my legs dangling over the edge. As we pass the shop, the black shape of a number eight appears under the truck and then slips away as we speed off. It stays on the road for weeks and each time we drive over it I remember the stars, and the feeling of being asleep in the fields, with the earth pressing up against me and the sky open on my face.

SPROUT

A sprout is a tender thing. Once its stem pushes aside the soil it has entered a different realm. The first leaves gather sunlight quickly so that the sprout thickens. Its color deepens. It reaches toward the light.

CHAPTER NINE

I began my semester by deep cleaning my half of the apartment. I laid out my clothing over the washed sheets, folding each pair of khakis, each cardigan and blouse in neat, bright squares. I scrubbed the dirt out of the skin on my knees and washed the last of the farm's sweat out of my hair. I still believed in second chances, in fresh starts. While Jayden slept off his hangover, I took his car downtown and bought art supplies and textbooks. I filled shopping bags with pens and notebooks, the regular stuff of hope. The city seemed brighter than I'd remembered it, having left in a late spring rain. Driving through campus to pick up my I.D., I couldn't help but feel excited for my classes, heavy doses of art and history. With my brushes and textbooks blocking my rear view window I began the semester with blind faith.

Jayden, on the other hand, began the semester with a steady diet of painkillers chased with the hardest alcohol he could find at the moment—wine, vodka, flammable rum, anything would do. He called it self-medication and the practice involved spending days gathering prescriptions from emergency rooms, pain clinics, and back alleys. One afternoon he received a package from a man he'd met on the beach in California, who'd sent him drugs from South America where the drugs were used for horses and cattle. Jayden thought they did better work on his back than any human drug a doctor would prescribe.

His schedule was dictated by pain. First, something would feel off, some ghost of discomfort in his nose or toe, or the deep-seated back ache, would suddenly flare into a life-threatening agony. Next, we'd have to find a way to fix the pain. I'd be hauled into the process out of concern or stop his rattling complaints. Sometimes I'd drive him to the emergency room where I'd sit in the lobby while, beyond sealed doors, he was passed from nurse, to doctor, to nurse again and would return, at least after the first few visits, proudly clutching a handwritten prescription. He'd walk taller, grinning, carrying that slip of hope. The pain would be gone for an hour, or a day, before it rose again at its own strange pace, growing not on any natural cycle, but in fits and starts. Again, he would be beholden to it and everything else—school, poetry, music—would fall away.

Some of the doctors came out to speak with me in the waiting room, looking both kind and sorry. They recommended exercise, physical therapy. Perhaps, they said, we could walk together, or try yoga. One man explained that the pain would go away with strength and stretching. Another wanted Jayden to see a chiropractor.

They all agreed that surgery was out of the question. The disc would just have to find its way back in line on its own. I saw the way Jayden glared at these doctors. He hated their advice, their fixes, their refusal to give him what he was searching for. Going home from the hospital empty-handed made his back worse. With his pain inflamed rather than healed by one of our fruitless hospital visits we'd stop at the liquor store, filling up on self-medication instead.

On weekend mornings I'd try to coax him out for a walk around our neighborhood or invite him downtown to stroll the farmers market. I lent him copies of my books on yoga and left my mat rolled up near his door. If he agreed to walk with me, he'd drag his feet and rant about how the doctors weren't giving him what he needed. His mood was like a storm, following us wherever we went, turning beautiful days dark. He hated the market, the smell of the fried foods, the colorful stalls. He hated the sun and the breeze. Everything that didn't numb him injured him.

A few weeks into the fall semester Jayden stopped waking in the morning to go to class. "I'm going," I'd call in the hallway. "I'm taking the car. Jayden can you hear me? I'm taking the car!" But nothing answered me. Just the heavy silence behind his closed door. Sometimes, if I came home during a midday break he'd be up and we'd drive together to afternoon classes, but most days he slept until the sunset and spent the nights rattling around the black box of a room, crashing away at the typewriter, hanging upside down from an inversion table which his mother had sent him for the pain, playing records until dawn.

My birthday fell late in October. I tried not to make a big deal about how lonely I felt in the moments when I was afforded a few moments of reflection. On my birthday I walked down from our apartment to the grocery store, through a small neighborhood park illuminated by streetlights, passing under huge evergreen trees, and around empty playgrounds. In the cold drizzle, I seemed like an exile from my own life. Outside, in the dark, cold dampness, all my bitterness left me, evaporating like fog into the rain. I imagined the night I could have been having at the farm, in the warm kitchen of The White House, with Creedence Clearwater pumping from the stereo, drinking dark beer and smoking cigarettes on the front steps, the frosty air seeping through my jeans as I looked out over the cut cornfield, toward the river, flowing like a ribbon of light behind dark bare oaks. I imagined Luke's laughter and Nick swaying very slightly to the music and Sarah's smile as she handed me a plate of roasted root vegetables she'd picked and cleaned and cooked herself.

But that place and those people were three thousand miles away. As I walked into the grocery store with hunched shoulders, shivering from the cold, my stomach began to growl. I found a big piece of cake, thick with pink frosting roses, and set it down with a candle shaped like Barbie at the register. I tried to smile at the cashier but she didn't look up from the transaction. *Happy Birthday*, I thought, bagging the cake and candle. Then I trudged back up the hill through the dark park, past bright windows and lit-up homes.

Before taking the climb up to our apartment I stopped by the bank of metal mailboxes. The rain pinged off them. It sounded hollow and sad, I thought. But inside, at the twist of the key, was a birthday card that everyone still working at the farm had signed—Sarah, Luke, Nick, Will and Kate—all their signatures scribbly and dear. There were even dirty thumb prints, whirling like little hurricanes at the edges. I pinned the card above my desk, opened as a butterfly so I could see each of their names whenever I looked up from the counter. They smiled at me there.

Jayden didn't come out of his room or make a sound as I locked up for the night. I flopped the cake onto a plate and stuck the huge candle deep into the frosting. The Barbie candle resembled a Hindu goddess in a relief carving—her head haloed with snaking hair, her pink lips slightly opened in a smile that could be the start of a prayer. I lit the wick and closed my eyes and like Dorothy I wished for just one thing that year: to go home.

In my old bedroom, in my parent's house, the late softness of October's early darkness settled like velvet over the pines, so that first the tree line, and then the field, vanished into dusk. I was going to bed early, preparing myself for a long day ahead. My dog, white around the muzzle, hiked the two flights of stairs to sleep with me, as she had for all my childhood nights when I'd lay in that bed and dreamed of being any place but there. The house felt small, like a tight sweater. The little valley with its collection of small towns didn't seem like the kind of setting where big things happened but that night, settling under the blankets, I was filled with anticipation. Tomorrow was a festival day at Cedar Circle when families crowded the pumpkin patch and horse-drawn wagons toured the fields. It was a public end to the season, the huge heavy fruits carried off the deadening earth, the last rush before the weather changed and the season's compass pointed towards stillness.

I woke up early under those familiar sheets before any light blushed the sky. I pulled wool socks up to my calves and buttoned up a pair of Carhartt jeans. I clipped my harvest knife on my belt and pinned my hair back, out of my face. Finally, sitting on the bottom step of the stairs I laced up my work boots and when I stood up, strong through the leg, as if rooted down.

As the day broke a gentle eggshell against the hillside's raw edges, I drove to the farm. A CD played Dylan live with the Band recorded on some thunderous evening just after he turned electric. During the previous summer, I had timed my bike commute by those tracks, slipping a portable CD player into my backpack so the music lay over the sounds of birds and the huffing of my breath. I knew each mile point and marked them in the car, counting down all the way to the turn to Vermont. The road took a left over a green metal bridge, rising above the water like the skeleton of some ancient beast, arched and riveted and guarded by a flock of pigeons that roosted in the barns along the river but spent their days high up on the bridge's crossbeams. When I biked across the birds would scatter and fly ahead of me, or burst out over the river, casting shadows on the shimmering waters.

The pigeons were still sleeping when I drove over the state line into Vermont. The river ran North-South dividing the land into neatly mapped sections. I always knew where I was when I was near the river.

The road came to a T by a gas station. The shop lights were already on, throwing shadows into the empty parking lot and a ragged cornfield. Without looking through the sliding glass doors I knew the face of the girl who opened early and set her baby to sleep behind the counter. Just past the gas station, the farm's sign stood like a cool white cross between the railroad tracks and the state highway. Its letters were hand painted in green and yellow. Another smaller sign, hammered into the gravel at the roadside read FESTIVAL SUNDAY.

The Pumpkin Festival flooded the farm's fields with locals and leaf-peepers, filling the parking lots with battered Subaru's and bumper-stickered Saabs as well as shining SUVs with New York and Massachusetts plates. Everyone who worked at the farm pitched in, the guys who drove tractors helped park cars, the girls who worked in the kitchen served cheesecake and the mechanics grilled local pork sausages. Families lay out on the big lawn in the shade of the red barn, waiting to have their kids' faces painted by girls had who picked strawberries and blueberries in the summer.

The morning of the Festival dawned soft and gray; the trees in the hedgerow faded to black at the corners of the property. I had gotten there early, long before the day started; I needed time to connect, to be in the place in peace before the rush of the crowds spilled over the rolling fields.

I left my car behind the big greenhouse where the earliest and latest tomatoes grew. As I walked by I peeked inside. The plants hung heavy and white with powdery mildew from bailing twine trellising but I could see a few red fruits hiding under those tired leaves. I shut the door tight against the cool morning and walked through the wet grass, past the dead shapes of the cut flower garden, the seed heads of rudbeckia and cosmos, the big disks of sunflowers pecked clean by little birds.

I hiked up the hill and over Pavilion Road, which separated the greenhouses from the barn and cut the farm in half. My boots left dew prints on the pavement. The farm stand had been decorated with cut corn stalks and bright gourds. Pumpkins of all shapes and colors sat on shelves and old apple crates; blue Cinderella's and yellow Cheddars, bright orange Magic Lanterns and striped Jaradahalls. Mums held dew on the tips of their simple flowers, bright-eyed in the shadow under the eaves. I brushed my hand over their faces.

Itchi the farm cat sat in the open doors of the barn, cleaning his paws, one toe at a time. I came up to him and knelt back on my heels and offered him my hand. He smelled it and didn't bolt and I knew I wasn't a stranger. He let me step over him into the barn and slipped out into the rustle of fallen maple trees scattered in the grass.

The air inside the barn was always colder. The barn had been built in the 1860s for dairy cows, although the stalls had also housed draft horses, pigs, chickens, and rabbits. Now our storage crops, towering stacks of white wax boxes filled with cured winter squash, onions, garlic, and potatoes filled each small room. I touched the worn handles of the hand tools, resting against the wall. My hoe hung in the back, it was the shortest one and fit me perfectly but anyone else would have to stoop to hold it. The blade gleamed sharply from the last time I ran a whetstone along its edge and sparked the steel into a point.

I walked the property taking the farm road down to the pumpkin patch, looping back up along the opposite edge of the field, listening to the slow awakening of the day, birds chattering, cars passing on the road, the chickens squawking as they laid their morning eggs.

The fields where I harvested squash and cucumbers all summer had been tilled up and turned over to the brown soil. The softer plants had collapsed in an early frost and lay limp on the raised beds. The strawberry patch had turned red and crispy; the straw between the aisles wasn't golden and shining anymore. Pumpkins were scattered on the crest of a hill that looked over the river. A big corn teepee hunched in the center of the patch. All of the farm's tractors were lined up in a neat row by the barn so kids could crawl on them. I loved the faces of the Farmall cubs the best, with their wide-set headlights like big cartoon eyes.

The soles of my boots filled with farm road dirt. I reached down and grabbed a handful of it and washed my hands dirty in the silt.

With the whirls of my fingerprints filled with soil and my boots thick with mud, I climbed the small hill up the back road behind the greenhouses, ready to meet the crew and begin our morning briefing. We were all marked by dirt and tan lines. I had known Luke, Nick, and Sarah for six seasons and I thought of them as my adopted family, we were like *The Lost Boys* or *The Boxcar Children*. In the fields, we told each other everything we thought we knew about ourselves, all of our stories, the funny ones and sometimes, after too many beers, in the heavy fog of a late night, all the sad ones too. We laughed and sweat and fought, and when we were very drunk, we cried together. Together we had harvested tons of potatoes and sorted the last of the dried onions. We'd clipped and hauled all the pumpkins from the fields at Alice's and scattered them on the home farm for Festival. We'd worked in mornings when the dew froze our fingers and then we'd sweat as the sun rose and our wool socks and heavy Carhartts dried stiff on our bodies.

As I walked through the mums and pumpkins around the farm stand, Nick and Luke, who lived in the white farmhouse, came across the road holding steaming mugs of coffee. Their faces were still dark but their lips had been chapped from the wind and cold. When I hugged them their sweatshirts smelled of soil and diesel. Nick dressed like a commando for Festivals, where he directed cars in the largest parking lot. He'd tucked camo-cargo pants into his high-polished logging boots and had his radio already in its holster. Luke's cheeks were freshly shaved and the rings in his ears looked chilly and bright. When I'd met him six years ago, he'd been sporting a blue mohawk. The mohawk was gone but he still blasted Rage Against the Machine while he washed vegetables in the produce area and kept the earrings in, six to an ear, stapled all along the edge.

Sarah ran over to meet us on the quiet farm road. We hugged and giggled and our giggling made our bodies vibrate like a bumblebee in a squash flower. She handed me a new sweatshirt with the farm's pumpkin logo printed on its chest and I slipped it over my flannel shirt so that we were all dressed in the farm's logo, a curling pumpkin vine weaving around a full, ribbed fruit.

I fell into step behind them as we walked down into the farm stand parking lot, watching Sarah's hips swing gracefully as a dancer. The familiar circle a tin of chew had worn through Nick's back pocket swayed as he stomped along. Luke moved confidently slightly ahead of everyone. He was our boss, our leader, the Field Manager. We were his crew.

Leaves lay in bright skirts under the old sugar maple by the Yellow House. As the sun rose, the barn cast a hard shadow that swept over the yard like a sundial. I helped toss table-clothes over the picnic tables and unfolded a stack of rented metal chairs. We threw bales of hay out in a circle for kids to sit on while they listened to a story-teller or to music. The kitchen staff fired up the grills and the air smelled like sausage and smoke.

The band pulled up and unloaded their instruments onto the old barn doors that served as our stage. They set up their speakers, while the singer rehearsed Old Crow Medicine Show covers into the crackling mic.

As the fog started to lift, I carried a cash box down to the shack in the pumpkin field where I'd work through the festival. I unlatched the door and propped open the piece of plywood that covered the front counter, set up a scale, organized pens and collected scratch paper. The shack became a clubhouse during strawberry season, where I holed up during busy days in June, weighing strawberry flats and collecting cash. There were doodles and graffiti inside from kids I didn't know who had worked in the shack thirty years ago. I'd hung my own artwork up too and my cell phone number was still taped to the wall, the paper wet and curling.

The shack had been dragged from the edge of the strawberry field and set up looking into the pumpkins. From the front counter, I could see the southern hedge-row and the farm road and beyond that, rows of dried cow corn in the neighbor's field. The corn rustled and crinkled in the wind. The band under the big tent by the barn continued to tune their instruments and those string plucks carried out to the shack too.

As I was finishing up cleaning, my Dad dropped off my youngest sister, Hannah, who got out of the passenger seat of his car and stretched. Her limps still seemed too long for her body and she complained always of being sore. Dad unpacked a breakfast of homemade pancakes and warm maple syrup for us, wrapped up in individual Tupperware containers. He'd rolled paper towels around plastic silverware and fixed us thermoses of tea, just the way we liked them, mine deeply brewed and black, Hannah's murky with milk and sugar.

Hannah and I sat together in our folding chairs behind the counter with billows of steam rising from our breakfast, pointing out the best pumpkins to each other before the festival began. We walked out and found a few good ones to display near the shack. Their rinds were cold and wet with dew. We set them up on the counter and then stepped back to admire our work.

Hannah was the baby of the family and easily everyone's favorite, including mine. I remembered holding her as an infant, changing her diapers, washing her puke out of my long hair, and feeding her with small, soft spoons. Having her by my side at the farm made me feel as tender towards her as I'd felt when she was small. When I'd left for boarding school Hannah was only eight years old, still a little kid. For a few years, I saw her only during breaks. We both grew up without each other. She'd become taller than me and smiled easily, while I tried to plaster fake grins on my lips.

There's a running joke in my family that I'm adopted; maybe that's why I never felt right with them. It wasn't that I was left out, it was that I didn't' belong there, to begin with. If you saw a picture of my family all lined up, I look like a visiting neighbor who happened to slip into the shot. My youngest siblings, Jake and Hannah are tall and blonde, with grey-blue eyes and bright smiles. My sister Elise, born two years after me, resembles our Mom. I am short and dark. In the summer, I tan deep olive from spending my time out in the woods or the fields.

Cherokee blood, Grammy said. But it wasn't just how we looked. It was a matter of character. I was always the wild one, impulsive and artistic. I slept under the stars. I ran away from home.

Sitting beside each other in the shack no one assumed we were sisters, but I sensed a deep connection to her when she worked with me at Cedar Circle. After all, farming is in my blood, the one thing that I held onto that tied me to my family. My grandfather had been a dairy farmer. He died during my Mom's senior year of high school, crushed by the trunk of an elm tree he was cutting in the cold of winter. In farming I believed I could reach back, it was my heritage. A green thumb, Mom said, skips a generation.

In the cool shade of the shack, Hannah and I sipped our tea. I wrote down the pumpkin pricing for her and tacked it to the wall near my strawberry notes from June and we watched as the first wagon ride took festivalgoers down the patch. The horse's harnesses jingled. Kids stood up on the seats and looked out at the fields of rye and late season spinach, carrots, and cabbage.

Suddenly, the sun parted the clouds and they hiked up their skirts and vanished into a high blue sky. The October afternoon blazed with color: red maples, yellow birches, browned oaks, grasses golden along the roadside and high into the soft hills. Families poured into the fields, searching through the pumpkins that sat brilliantly orange in a bed of bright green oats.

Smells rose with the heat, sweet rotting pumpkin, fresh, trampled grass, dark river water, rich soil, cider from plastic cups, maple syrup on our fingers from break-fast, sticky dollar bills and metallic coins, staining our hands with the bitter smell of money. We instructed the pumpkin pickers to form two lines, one in front of each of us and didn't stop smiling or talking through the whole early Festival rush.

Working the pumpkin shack was simple, but we had to be quick. As people waited their pumpkins grew heavy in their arms and their kids got grumpy, couples started to bicker and scroll through their phones bitterly so we moved everyone along as fast as possible. When a group reached the counter they'd hand off all their pumpkins up to us and we'd quickly wipe the blossom ends off with a damp towel. Carefully, we'd balance as many pumpkins as possible on the scale to save time then multiply the weight by the price per pound on a calculator. We'd snap open the cash box and hand out change, or write up a slip if they wanted to pay up in the farm stand, with a credit card. Then, gingerly, we'd pass the pumpkins back down to the family and sweep the scale clean of dirt and smile at the next group and begin the whole process again.

During breaks in the line, I took pictures of Hannah posing behind the counter, pictures of her walking in the pumpkin field or helping a customer, selfies of the two us lounging, with cups of steaming mulled cider, the sun in our eyes, squinting as we smile.

The light in October drained away quickly. By four o'clock the sun shifted to the west, dipping beneath the hills and without ringing any bell, or calling over a loud-speaker, everyone knew the Festival was over. Pumpkins were packed into trunks, kids snapped into car seats and the roads filled one last time with a stream of exiting traffic. The farm became quiet again.

As the temperature dropped I counted out the big bills in the cash box and surveyed the pumpkin patch, now mostly empty. Little feet had pounded the grass down and the corn teepee stood at a slight angle, battered by climbing children. Shadows stretched out long over the fields giving the pumpkins and plants spooky reflections.

Hannah and I picked up trash, carried the cash box up to the yellow house and shut down the shack for the season. We made sure the boxes of quarts stood tall, and that the latch on the front end was closed tight. Shutting the door one last time I felt like I was tucking a child into bed. The musicians went home and the last insects took up their metallic hum in the trees. As the kitchen staff cleaned dishes, I could hear them talking and singing to the radio as the plates clinked in the big metal sinks. The farm stand crew closed up and drove away into the night, lowering the garage doors, which faced the road like shut eyelids. Dad took Hannah home; she waited for him by the big maple tree, with a pumpkin at her feet.

I helped fold up table clothes and pack up chairs. We hauled hay bales back to the loft above the horse barn and swept off the stage. One by one headlights vanished into the night until only Sarah, Luke, Nick, and I remained. We ordered a pizza from town and waited for it to be delivered, sitting on the tailgate of the farm truck, watching lights across the river in New Hampshire. We were mostly quiet, our cheeks sore from smiling. Every day in high summer ended just like that, sitting or leaning on the truck, looking into the same distance, thinking the same thoughts. It was groupthink. Telepathy.

After Pumpkin Festival we imagined the fields which were too dark to see, the shack and the orchard fence, and how empty the ground lay now, how peaceful. When the pizza arrived we ate quickly in the darkness of the barn under one light bulb, drinking warm beer. It was easy to imagine that we were the only people in the world, the space beyond us all shadow and mystery. The barn filled with its night energy, its odd sleeping sense of time, creaking and moaning. Maybe it was the sound of animals crawling out of the foundation or settling in the rafters, or the muttering of ghost farmers as they shuffled around at chores, or just old wood and ancient stone adjusting to the cold night air.

Under the stars we lit cigarettes and leaned back onto the barn boards, smoking in silence, sharing that cold, October night without saying a word.

The house lights across the river went dark. It was getting late. Our breath hung in low clouds in the barn's floodlight. Our hands were cold and pink in our pockets and our cigarette packs lay limp and empty. The last of the beer bottles was tossed in the recycling bin where it tolled like a bell. Sarah left first, yawning and rubbing her blue eyes. I hugged her hard like I wanted to press some of her loveliness onto my arms and carry it home bright and sweet as a bouquet. Then Nick and Luke headed back across the road, flicking their cigarettes in the trash and saluting me goodbye.

Then the farm was quiet. The fields lay open in the moonlight, and the river beyond shown like a path. I drew the moment out as long as I could, saying goodbye until I was alone, under the light bulb. *Goodbye,* I said, *I'll see you again soon,* to no one in particular, to the place, to the fields and river and silty roads.

Jayden woke me. He flicked the light on in the kitchen. It was some hour between night and day, too early to be up and too late to be going back to sleep. The window outside was black. I squinted at him and sat up in bed.

"I can't feel my nose," he said, and then repeated the same phrase like a mantra, as if the words had no meaning and were spoken only to be rolled on the tongue.

"What?" I muttered, unfolding from the warmth of the bed and setting my feet on the carpet.

"I can't feel my nose!" In the light of the kitchen, I could see that his face was white with fear, his eyes were wild, he was sweating a thin sheet of gloss over his nose and cheeks. I couldn't tell if he was high, or in pain, or both.

"What should we do about it?" I asked. It was a weekend morning and I had the day open to tend to him at least. Homework could wait until the evening. In my head I made minor adjustments to my reading plan, figured the hours spent researching, the hours spent writing, and then tried to come back to the kitchen. The tile was cool. The kitchen's pink paint was sharp in my vision. Jayden was pacing back and forth, back and forth, bumping into the counter then bouncing to the wall like a pinball trapped in a machine.

"I don't know," he cried. I could hear in his voice the hard edge of terror. He was scared of his body, of its mechanisms and breaks. I thought I knew what he was most frightened of but we never spoke of such things. At one time I could have laid his thoughts out clearly, like an archaeologist excavating items onto a tarp and giving each its value, history, and purpose. But through the drugs and the separation, there was nothing but speculation and fog. I thought he feared losing his mind. All the phantom pains and their mirrored numbness seemed to me like ghosts of this fear. They were the physical representations of his loss of control. Like a car's nonessential parts breaking down before the engine failed. It seemed that bit by bit Jayden's body was falling to pieces.

He paced as if the world was closing in on him like a trapped animal, rubbing his face, trying to feel something. The sheen of sweat on his checks thickened and I could smell it radiating—the fear, the sickness. Our cat watched him like she watched birds through the glass, her eyes tracking his path across the kitchen floor. I promised him I'd take him to the emergency room. I didn't know what else to do. What did you treat ghost pain with? What if the nerves everywhere were breaking in him? I zipped up a sweater and stuffed my feet into a pair of rain-damp boots. Light was spreading sick and grey over the eastern crown of the Cascades.

In the car Jayden poked at his nose, waiting for it to respond to his touch. I watched him as warily as the cat had. Something had bloomed in me recently that made me concerned for his safety. I locked the sliding glass door at night, hoping that he'd be too drunk to figure out the mechanism. I poured vodka down the sink. I'd started hiding his keys in the freezer. When I was in class and he was at home I sat and wondered if he'd be alive when I got back. He might jump out of the moving car. I locked the doors as we pulled onto the interstate. Anything felt possible.

In the emergency waiting room, the hospital lights fell hard on his face. I'd stopped caring how I looked when I went out. If Jayden was with me minding him took all my attention. I was sure my hair hung ragged, in need of a trim, a few days past clean, my face unwashed, oily from sleep. I was hastily dressed in jeans and a sweater, not the organized girl I usually was in public. I'd started to break apart into smaller pieces. I'd stopped thinking of myself at all. Jayden filled me as he had when we were in love. Except this was love's sick twin. Something both maternal and pitiful. But at least it was something, I thought; at least I had a role in his life.

The lights buzzed and a TV screen played the local news soundlessly. Jayden moaned and twisted his fingers together. He shifted his back in the plastic chair. I held my purse in my lap and looked straight ahead, to the door where someone would come and take him away. A nurse called his name and he shuffled towards her and the door took both of them out of sight. I sat there waiting. I had nothing with me to read. I had nothing at all. I tried to think about the essay I planned to write that afternoon but the order of my thoughts was tangled and weedy. I dragged myself back to the hospital, to my body, to Jayden.

I heard him yelling before I saw him.

"Fuck you," he was shouting. "Fuck you, you fraud!" A tall man was walking him out by the elbow. Jayden was twisted at the waist, looking back at a doctor who was following him out into the waiting room. The nurse who'd taken him away was there too, standing behind the doctor like back up. Jayden's cheeks were red. The face of the man leading him was distant as the moon, but the doctor's eyebrows crashed together over his hard eyes and he shook his head bitterly.

I clutched my purse and stood up. I felt very small. Like a seed you could hardly see, let alone hold between two fingers. The security guard let go of Jayden and gave him a nudge towards me, then he crossed his arms over his broad chest and planted his feet wide, forming a body wall between Jayden and the medical staff. He didn't look upset, just serious.

"Fuck this place," Jayden spat, storming past me and out the sliding doors. He walked faster and stronger than I'd seen him walk in weeks, as if the rage overwhelmed the pain. I looked up, hoping that I'd be offered some sort of treatment plan, but the doctor glared at me as he had at Jayden. "If you pill-seeking kids ever come back here, I'll have you escorted off the property," he said from behind the right shoulder of the security guard.

"Sorry?" I murmured, confused.

"You're banned. His name's on the list. You can't get your fix here."

"But his nose?" I asked.

The doctor laughed and the nurse smiled a nasty little smirk. "How much cocaine was he doing last night? Hmm?" I stared at him. Had Jayden been doing coke? I had no idea. He'd been in the back room since I returned from my evening lecture. I didn't realize that I looked as messy and sick as Jayden, my face naked and unwashed, my clothing pulled from the laundry bin in a hurry. I didn't think that I'd been seen as anything other than his caretaker. I was so embarrassed that I bowed my head and offered some murmured apology which I'm sure none of them were able to hear. I kept my eyes on my boots as I rushed out, feeling their judgment hot on my back. Tears stung my eyes. I wanted to sit alone and cry. The shame was so infectious, so horribly itchy and I wanted to expel it, to wash it out of me.

It was a dim morning with rain starting to fall in blowing wisps. There was still bright color in the leaves but the clouds hung low, hiding the hills and distant mountains. Jayden was standing against his car, his back hunched again like a question mark. He shook his head, rattling his curls. "Those assholes," he was saying, sucking furiously on a cigarette, his finger shaking as he knocked ash onto the pavement.

"Jayden," I began and then paused, ashamed at my lack of faith, ashamed at how little I knew about the boy I had once loved. "Were you doing coke?"

"Fuck, you believe them too?"

"I don't know . . . I just. Your nose?"

"I woke up and couldn't feel my nose. Just like I told you. Just like I told them." He started to cry. He was telling the truth. I remembered his fear in the early morning, his frightful pacing in the kitchen and I knew he was thinking of that numbness working its way back through his nose into his skull, settling blankly on his brain, freezing the words, stopping up the poetry, paralyzing him forever.

I told him I was sorry for even asking, that I believed him, because in some ways I did. I believed in a part of the pain if not the specific pain. I believed in the bigger problem which seeded its own universe of pain. I believed that he was sick and hurting and that it seemed like now I was the only one who could care for him.

I took him out for breakfast at our favorite diner which had once been a strip club. "My treat," I said, opening the door for him. The smell of cigarette smoke and hot grease washed over us. The diner owners had kept the purple velveteen circular booths but had turned the mirrored walls into windows looking out on a broken-down mall and the busy road flowing dimly into the city. We sat across from each other, ragged and worn. The taste of sugar and fat drew me back into life. We ate like we'd been fasting, dragging pancakes through syrup and sausage grease, smearing jam on buttered toast, drinking hot chocolates smothered in whipped cream. I couldn't look at him across the table. It wasn't just his face that scared me, it was the sight of myself, reflected back in his gold-green eyes: a ghost girl, haunting my skin.

꙳

As the last lights dim, the water inside the leaf cells freeze. As they harden, they expand ever so slightly, breaking up the borders that form their structure. When the sun rises, and the chill fades, the leaves go soft. They fall limp over the rows. The frost bruises the leaves dark as black eyes. Walking the field, I can find the low spots where the night bit hardest. Only the toughest plants survive: the waxy Brassicas, broccoli, cabbage and cauliflower, kale and collard greens. Even though the spinach has frozen, it thaws and wilts then grows plump again, a winter variety, planted so we can pick it through the fall.

In a night the quilt of the field changes. Mostly it fades to brown. Green belts of blue remain but suddenly it is a different landscape. Just like most of the staff leaves in August, bringing their cheer, noise and laugher with them, in September, the first hard frost takes away the diversity of summer and its many colors. Gone are the sweet basil, the crisp lettuce, the spicy arugula, and snappy bush beans. No more squash or cucumbers, the flower garden hangs limp as a faded bouquet, and the corn turns black along the edges.

The flavors of fall are built on the density grown for months, accumulating a history of sunlight and rainstorms. We roast potatoes, shallots, winter squash, onions, garlic, blood-red beets, white fingers of parsnips and the sweet storage carrots. They taste of soil and age, accumulating flavor as they sit in wax boxes and in the walk-in coolers as if the very process of thinking back and remembering turned their starch to sweet sugars.

The fall feeds off my moodiness, the many small deaths gather into a general sense of loss. I watch the things I have grown from seed, from hands and water and soil, go soft and then die. I pull the tomatoes from the greenhouses, cutting them off their strings and carting them down to the compost piles. I remember their huge fruits, striped like golden rainbows and as soft as a lover's breast. I thank each plant.

If I work alone, I whisper it out loud: *Thank you for starting small and growing above my head. Thank you for having roots so deep they reached out and found groundwater. Thank you for turning the fundamental chemistry of the world into food.*

Thank you for opening your flowers to the bees, for the small yellow beginnings of tomatoes. Thank you for your fluorescent green pollen that covered my arms and hands and made me remember, at the end of the day, that I tended to the vital things in this world.

I say this as I cut them to pieces.

On harvest day, I pick spinach by myself in the hoop house. No crew, just my own body, inching over the earth. Rain falls lightly. Inside, the plastic skin acts as a drum, making even the smallest shower sound like a raging downpour. The rest of the world disappears. Water trickles down the sides and fogs up the view out to the road and the farm stand. The spinach froze in the night and lies hard and brittle, flat against the beds. It might look dead but it's only resting. I know that the leaves will thaw in the coolers and the next day the greens will be plumb again and ready to be washed and bagged without bruising. Using my thumb and pointer finger I snap off the brittle stems and toss each leaf gently into a bushel basket. If I am rough with the spinach it will turn soft and break as it warms.

The ground is hard under my knees. I shuffle forward in tiny steps through the aisle, trying to find a comfortable place to kneel. I can feel the cold biting through thick canvas pants and long underwear. My right hand is numb from touching the frozen plants but I need my fingers bare to pick the spinach. My left is gloved and clings to the bushel basket for support as I walk on my knees down the length of the planting. Time doesn't matter anymore. It can take the whole morning to pick the spinach by myself. What matters is that it gets picked, so hours and minutes slide away into circular thoughts and daydreams.

Will, the farm's owner, startles me by opening the doors at the far end of the hoop house. I haven't heard him approaching. He is wearing sweatpants and a cotton sweatshirt; his feet are slipped into flip-flops despite the cold and his long white hair is loose of its braids, hanging around his shoulders. A thick white stubble covers his jaw and adds depth to his smile lines. He grins and his happiness at finding me there, working the farm quietly, reminds me of how he had once told me about the magical hidden world in the soil, how it revolves around creatures too small to see, and the particles forged at the creation of the universe. He is a spiritual leader; more than a manager, charged with the sort of the eclectic passion that drives a person to act rather than forces them to hurry up, or pick faster. This morning, on my birthday, I love him easily.

He kneels beside me in the row, his blue eyes swimming in glossy tears, the cold stinging. He holds my hand between his and presses firmly. "We love you sister," he says. "You do so much for us. Happy birthday." Will reaches into his pocket and draws out a bronze statue of Ganesh, the elephant god, and presses its heavy weight into my hands.

"He'll bring you good luck."

As soon as I thank him, he is up and walking away, back to his study by the fireplace in The Yellow House. I set the statue on the row in front of me and continue my harvest. I recognize it quickly from the mantel in their house and know that Will had picked it out when he realized it was my birthday. All the same, I imagine that years ago he'd found it in a market in India, where he and Kate traveled often. Their house is full of images of Ganesh— the pot-bellied, elephant-headed god of good fortune. You are supposed to rub his belly for good luck so their metal statues' bellies shine bright as new pennies. In his four arms, he holds goblets and bells and he lounges on a chaise with one leg folded comfortably, draped in silks and necklaces. The elephant god looks at me peacefully from the aisle in the hoop house. Life is good, he seems to say. Good luck. Fortune. Plenty. These are the realms of Ganesh. While other Hindu deities hold sickles and swords or dance with the skulls of the dead around their waists, Ganesh is cheerful, fat, and peaceful. I reach out with my frozen finger and rub his potbelly. The metal is already cold.

CHAPTER ELEVEN

Each time we went out looking for a cure I grew a little away from the sun, stretching out like a long thin shadow of my old self. My bones felt heavy. Most days I slept lightly, afraid to wake to find Jayden prying open the sliding glass door or slicing through the air with a kitchen knife. I slept and lived in the constant presence of fear.

By late October I could draw a constellation of pain clinics around the city limits. I remembered which ones were nice to us and which had put Jayden on their no-sell list. I also knew which pharmacies were open 24 hours and which closed at 6:00, or 9:00 P.M. I knew the address of a kind back pain specialist who invited me into Jayden's appointment and showed me the disc on his MRI scan so that when I imagined his pain, I pictured that curved question mark of the bone, with one knuckle pushed slightly farther out than all the others. That doctor recommended stretches and handed Jayden a printout of different exercises. Jayden had crumpled it up in the car.

We never went back there again because he didn't give Jayden what he was looking for. He didn't write him a prescription.

Each week the constellation of pain clinics grew dimmer. Every repeat visit crossed a name off the list. One night we drove to three clinics, all of which were closed, and to one emergency room, where he was refused medication, and all night I knew that what I was doing was useless and potentially harmful, making him worse rather than better. But at least I was doing something. We were out of the apartment. We were moving. And there wasn't much else for me to do. I couldn't sleep while he wept, or raged or drank himself to blackout in front of the TV; I couldn't study, call home, take a shower. That one late night when every clinic was closed and the city itself seemed to be shuttered to us, we ended up at a Denny's, fifty miles away from home, drinking oil-stained coffee in the witching hours with long-haul truckers and addicts. Men who itched their arms as they ate. Women with shadows under their eyes like eclipsed moons.

We sat through several cups of coffee, plates of burgers and fries, and soupy milkshakes. I could hardly look at him anymore. A collapse had arrived on his face, like autumn to the forest. Beauty fell from him. All I could see anymore were the bones of his structure. Gone were the schoolboy eyes, the pink cheeks, the chapped lips stained with ink from sucking on the ends of pens. Gone were the light curls, the sunny freckles, the fuzz along his jaw, peachy and nearly white. Jayden was a shell, a husk like stripped corn, left in the last fields of fall.

"I think I'm going to die," he said, sucking at the last puddle of milkshake. He told me this nearly every day. Death perched on his shoulder, lurking just around the corner of dawn.

"No, you'll get better. You'll heal," I said, as I always said. We'd fallen into the trapped streams of repeated conversations. Again and again the same questions. The same statements. I told him about the MRI, the stretches, the process of time, how it would work within him, how it would mend him. I told him to hold out, to hope. I couldn't let go of the idea. If things weren't getting better then what was I doing? What could you do without the promise of a sunrise or the coming of summer? But sitting there, licking salt from my fingers, with the overhead light glaring strange in the depth of the night, I wondered why we were even here. I wondered if at some point everything good would dry up and I'd be left alone with nothing. I'd started reserving my strength for these nights. Sleeping late when I could. Showering when he was sleeping. Running errands if he was at the library. Preparing for the worst.

It wasn't love. That was just a few good memories that I wore smooth as beach stones.

It wasn't hope. He'd burnt through any of that months ago. I knew by then that he wasn't going to come back from this. I knew we would never be what we were if we remained anything at all. But his habits had become dangerous and I had shifted into the role of guardian and nursemaid.

Jayden had defined my world for four years, giving

it borders and destinations. I knew myself in relation to him. And before Jayden, there was another boy and before him, there was the dark selflessness of middle school when I didn't know who I was or wanted to be. Being a girlfriend was my specialty. I excelled at it. I was patient and shifting like a chameleon. I was quick to change how I dressed, what books I read, where I liked to eat and travel and what drugs or drinks I preferred. I was happier being an us, happier in a pair. At least now we were linked again, chained to the same grim future.

What scared me more than the thought of Jayden hurting himself was the thought of being nothing, of having no one.

I threw out his pills at night.

I poured gin and vodka down the sink. I hid his keys.

I made him sandwiches and pasta and eggs to soak up the booze. I cleaned up his vomit. I washed his greasy laundry.

One night I called the police to search for him when he'd found his keys and rushed out, tripping down the stairs and peeling out of the parking lot.

"A black VW Jetta with California plates," I said over the phone. "Driving under the influence. A danger to himself and others."

I went out looking for him, circling the apartment complex, hunting the empty campus lots. Rain was beating on my windshield. It was the middle of the night and all the houses along the road were dark. At every turn, I thought I'd see his car smashed into a spruce trunk, or flipped over a guardrail. I braced myself for it.

My cell phone rang and I jumped at the noise as if it signaled Jayden's accident. It was the campus police. The night librarian had requested their assistance. Jayden was found weeping in the poetry section, tearing books off the shelf, holding them to his chest, lying on them as if they were pillows. When I got to campus, he was sitting in one of their cruisers. The rain on the window washed out his face.

I took him home and drew him a bath.

I woke up early the next morning for class; my shoes still cold from the night's rain and my eyes raw from tears. I thought if I saw myself in a mirror, I might be transparent, like a ghost or an onion skin.

I couldn't talk about what I was doing for Jayden when my mother asked, how bad he was getting as the days thinned out into November. All of our calls went blank and I ended up inventing some reason I had to say good-bye. I realized that I was embarrassed by our life more than anything, the day-to-day shuffle of it between points of pain. I was ashamed that I cared for him, ashamed that we still lived together, broken and sick. Somehow, I communicated to my parents that he wasn't going to class and if he was gone, I had no way to drive to campus. A year ago when Jayden and I found our apartment, we hadn't thought to look at city bus lines, assuming that we'd always have each other, side by side. But now I found myself trapped on a hill outside of the rings of public transportation, miles from campus, without a car.

In an act of incredible trust and compassion my father bought a new car over the phone. It was, he promised, really for my mother. Since my old Subaru was resting in the driveway back in New Hampshire I was to drive the new car home in May as a birthday present for my mother who was the legal owner on the title that I was to save in a thick envelope. I promised to keep the car clean, to make sure it arrived safe and free of scratches, my voice breathless over the phone. When the salesman from the dealership appeared in his shiny rental car, I felt for the first time in weeks like a real person. It wasn't that I didn't eat or get dressed on any other day but on this one I felt solid. I wasn't part of the world of ghosts anymore. My heels clicked down the stairs joyfully. The salesman got out and opened the door for me and for the few minutes that it took to drive from my apartment to the dealership, we talked about nothing at all, just the everyday chatter of two normal people. The car was clean and smelled like air freshener. The radio played pop hits that I'd half-forgotten, low, like a stream running under our chitchat. I'd dressed up for the occasion and painted my lips a confident pink. My hair was clean and hung lightly by my jawline. When they handed me the keys and led me through the lot, I could see myself passing in the mirror finishes of station wagons and SUVs. I shook their hands, slipped the title into the envelope as my father had instructed and pulled the latch. The air inside was factory fresh, almost choking with plastic sweetness. For days I kept the paper floormats and plastic seat covers, reveling in the newness, the niceness of the interior space. It was just a car of course, but it was also a thing that was distinctly mine.

I started to live for Thanksgiving. I'd invited my farm friends Sarah and Nick out to Portland for the holiday. We'd agreed on the trip months earlier before my life there with Jayden was an embarrassing ruin, and I was too ashamed to tell them that we were a mess. Instead, I'd call Sarah and we'd prepare a list of dishes for our Thanksgiving table: roots from the farm, roasted sticky sweet. Hearing her voice bubble from the phone made the flatness of my days all the stranger. I wanted to reach out to her, to the farm, but I also could think of nothing but hiding. I felt, somehow, like a failure. She knew that Jayden and I had gone through some sort of breakup but I'd left it there as I had in the summer, open to mending, to growing, to starting again. Sarah was brightly optimistic in all things, always nursing the sickest plants, taking home warped vegetables too ugly for anyone else, leaving saucers of cream for stray cats along the hedgerow like offerings to small gods. I wanted Sarah to believe that Jayden and I were happy. We could pretend to be okay, I thought, for three days.

In our apartment, I didn't have a door to close. I slept openly, in the shared living space where the kitchen, hallway, patio and front door met. We shared pots and pans, plates and knives, a shower, a laundry basket. I stopped cooking elaborate meals. I didn't explore the state on weekends or hike in the rainforests but I still managed to keep up with my course work. I went to class as I always had, arriving early and leaving last. Sitting behind the table, or in a library booth, I looked like a normal girl. Pushing reading glasses up the bridge of her nose.

Taking notes. And maybe in those moments, everything was all right. Maybe I was holding it all together even if I felt hollowed out inside, as bare as a watermelon rind.

❦

At the farm October is a month of color, then nothing but grey. Grey from the stone walls as they appear in the barren woods. Grey from the trunks of wet birch, oak, and maple. Grey from the soggy old leaves. Grey from clapboards and roads leading into grey forests, through valleys of grey hills. The sky is heavy with clouds that have no definition, just a flat heavy grey like newsprint. The foliage fades quickly. Rain brings the leaves down. First, they are brilliant on the ground, carpets of gold and crimson more saturated than fibers in the finest Persian rugs, but the rain keeps coming and flattens them and the color drains as the earth becomes one tone.

The river runs dark too, full of runoff and of shadows from the grey trees and the gloomy hills. The pumpkins stand out like targets in the field but not many people want to walk out to pick them in the mud. The ones near the farm stand sell first. Then, during breaks in the weather, families dart down to the patch and haul up big jack-o'-lanterns in the old, whining Red Flyer wagons, warming their hands with cups of hot cider in the cold breath of the farm stand. They quickly leave with the fading light.

I remember working in that dimness, another fall years ago, between high school and college. Unlike this one it was full of soaring blue skies and bright yellow leaves well into the end of the month. The mornings were pretty, frost formed ice jewelry on leaves and along the rims of puddles. Geese zipped up the sky in great Vs, following the course of the river down to the seaboard and then farther to the temperate south. The crew waved at them like relatives leaving after Thanksgiving dinner.

See you soon! Have a good winter! The greens in the fields held strong and bright even though the shadows crept up early like friendly cats.

But Octobers are always different. The seasons of transition in New England can swing quickly; October can be brilliant or bitter, just as April can be bright or frigid. The rain grows rot and the rot moves through the fields quickly. First the hoop house tomatoes. Then the last of the Brassicas. The lettuces already softened by the frost are pressed to the soil, beaten translucent by the rain. The weather speeds up the season until, very soon, the end has come.

Now the fields are nearly empty. The hoop houses have been stripped and replanted into winter greens. The barn is cleaned and set for the cold. Potatoes, squash, onions, and garlic are stacked high in wax boxes, cleaned and sorted and waiting for the slow sales of the last few weeks. Carrots, beets, and parsnips grow cool and sweet in the walk-ins. The crew breaks apart, slowly, one person drifting off to part-time and then away for good. Some of them never come back. By the end of the month, only Nick, Luke, and I remain.

Even in my happiest years, the fall is hard to bear. Some days I feel the busy energy of cleaning and organizing, prepping for a new season. Those days are full of dreams and promises but they always hinge on the future. In the present, the jobs are more about endings. Stripping out plants, emptying greenhouses, laying off staff, tilling under fall plantings until the fields are blank pages again. Finally, we blow out the pipes so that even the busy, clear water will stop pulsing through the many veins that connect the well to the barn and greenhouses, lines strung up through the rafters and buried in the ground and always, quietly, running.

In October the silence is startling. The cooling and vent fans in the big greenhouses are unplugged for the season. There is no traffic to the farm stand, no rumbling gravel as cars pull in and out, no kids squealing as they drag wagons around the grass yard, no doors opening and slamming as customers come and go from the coffee shop.

Most days only Yoda rolls around the farm, so the symphony of squeaking struts and grinding gears from the other old farm trucks are absent. The tractors, unless they are disking or plowing up a planting, don't roar as they start, or chug along through the soil. And the voices are gone. No girls singing in the strawberries. No Robert and Luke laughing about something in the shed. No Nick trying to call Itchi out of the chicken coop. No music from the big speakers in the processing area or from the fizzy sound systems in the trucks. No swearing or shouting down to the end of a 600-foot row. No storytelling low in the shade of deep weeds. No whistling, humming or two-way radio chatter.

Even the wind settles. With no leaves on the trees, the world is quieter. The corn plantings have been mowed and no longer rustle like skirts. Some days all I can hear is the drip of rain. In the silence, there is the cold heart of the coming winter. Like an unspoken thing. Real as heartbreak.

The ghosts in the barn settle too and the place feels deserted by all human memory. I imagine them tucking back into their graves on the cemetery just up the road for the winter, like retired people flying to Florida for the snowy months. And the animals, the great draft horses that once worked the silty fields, roll back into the holes at the base of the hill near the barn where they were buried centuries ago.

At first, the living animals are busy—collecting nuts, crafting nests—and then, suddenly, on some deep, cold night near the end of the month they begin to sleep as well. The skunks fall into hibernation in their hollows under the barn's foundation stones. Chipmunks curl in the walls and their clatter, their biting calls, are just a memory too. It is only when they are gone that I realize how loud they were.

In October I put things away and move on. I have to acknowledge that the season is over. There is no faking it. I've been filled then emptied again. The big plants that I had started as seeds, transplanted, weeded around and picked are now brush hogged into mush and then flipped over to rot in the belly of the earth. Those days in June and July—when we swung our dirty feet into the warm river water, when I biked through tender foggy sunrises, when my sister Hannah smiled at me from the strawberry shack, and I sprinted between harvest and planting—those days are done.

CHAPTER TWELVE

My body seemed to need a lot of water and light in November, as if was trying to sprout. Jayden wore at me like sand shaping sea glass. The Portland rain washed me out, that slick damp season so different than the bitter grey of a New England November. The rain ran steadily down our chimney, it poured like tears over the windshield of my car. At night it brushed gently on the roof of the apartment building, making just enough noise to keep me awake.

In those rainy dim days I was just a pinprick, a black point, as small in the palm as a broccoli or cabbage seed, slightly shiny and light enough to blow away. Inside that seed was an image of a farm girl and I clung to it when I couldn't remember who I was. It was a memory from four summers ago, a moving picture from a time when I felt comfortable in my skin. I was standing barefoot on a cool cement slab under the overhanging roof of the barn. It was after work, and the rest of the field crew were already drinking beers and tossing horseshoes behind the farmhouse.

In the memory, I could hear horseshoes ringing off the stake. I was cleaning our small garlic harvest and didn't want to quit until it was finished. I was trying to prove myself, but no one was taking note. It was mid-August. I knew that I was leaving soon. Those days, those final weeks, were always more beautiful, enriched by a powerful sense of loss.

The garlic was spread out in front of me on a round table, and I was cutting the roots and the stem and then coaxing the dirty layers of skin off with my thumb. There was a big storm rising to the west, one of those afternoon thundershowers of late summer, nearly black as it boiled up to the top of the world. Everything lay quiet before it. I heard the walk-in coolers humming. I heard traffic on the road, the sounds of the birds in the rafters, the chickens in their coop, Itchi stalking the gravel driveway. I was this barefoot girl, tan and dirty, and I thought, I am glad to be her. I kept going back to savor the image.

At the end of November, Nick and Sarah flew out from Vermont to celebrate Thanksgiving with me. Nick had never been on an airplane before and he arrived, stumbling in his logging boots through the vast sunlit halls of the Portland airport, guided by Sarah with her angelic smile. They smelled like woodsmoke and snow. I couldn't get enough of them. I hugged them and hugged them again when we picked up their baggage and, in the car, I just wanted to sit and feel their energy fill that space. They were electric. Although the city lay flat and dark, I took the long way to our apartment through downtown so that they could see the tight streets, the winged bridges, the cold strong river, a city of old brick, and new glass shining. They pressed their faces to the car windows, fogging up the view and I felt like I belonged again, to something.

In the apartment, I'd deep-cleaned Jayden's room so that it no longer smelled like his unwashed hair and piles of dirty laundry. I'd left a candle in there, burning away the gloom, and it had filled the space with an intoxicating fake lilac scent. Earlier that morning I'd dressed the inflatable mattress in pretty sheets and tried to disguise a collection of camping mats as a second bed on the floor, piling pillows up against the nearby wall like a headboard. Jayden insisted on leaving up his poster of the two women kissing, but he'd taken his record player back into the main room along with his typewriter. He set both down on the floor beneath a long slice of a window which overlooked the street and was our cat's favorite lookout space. When we returned, he was sitting cross-legged on the carpet like a yogi, typing, as the cat chased strikers across the page. He'd showered and changed into clean clothing and as he unfolded his long body to meet them he looked, I thought, healthy and warm.

Nick and Sarah set their things in the back room and that night, tired and jetlagged, we ordered in Thai and slurped up our noodles in front of the TV. I kept looking at them to make sure they were still there, as if they might dissolve into the air. Sarah and Nick were the figures in my daydreams, the faces in the pictures on my walls, and now they were here filling the space with light. To hear their laughter ring in my apartment brought me back to the tight breath of the barn, or the cab of Yoda, where, on cold mornings, all three of us would pack in, with me straddling the gear shift, my hips pressed between their hips. In Portland, I wanted to be just as close to them. That night they slept in the back room, Sarah on the air mattress and Nick on camping mats on the floor. I lay awake listening, as if the air in the apartment was altered by their presence. Jayden shared the big bed in the living room with me but we slept on opposite ends and recoiled if we rolled inward toward each other.

We woke on Thanksgiving morning and while a parade marched across the TV screen, I flipped pancakes in the kitchen. Jayden and Nick talked soccer and Sarah read a book of poetry at the countertop bar. Her round face and Peter Pan haircut made her look like a cherub. As I cooked, I glanced over my shoulder at them. Nick and Sarah. The field crew. Here, in my apartment. How easy it was to talk and move again, how light I felt pouring maple syrup in the pitcher. The press of what I'd been carrying lifted from me. Jayden, too, appeared to blossom under their attention. Not only had he washed his face and brushed his hair but he was also standing straighter and his eyes were clear again, those shining yellow emeralds that I'd first fallen in love with. We sat out on the porch, despite the bite in the air. As if on cue the great skirts of the clouds rose up and revealed Mount Hood's white summit, shimmering in the clear sky. Nick and Sarah rushed to get their cameras and I took their photo, leaning against the backdrop of the city, the mountain white against blue, their smiles big as moons. They made the place beautiful again for me.

Hidden in her suitcase Sarah had smuggled bags of potatoes, onions, carrots, and garlic. She'd wrapped butternut squash in T-shirts and packed Ball jars of pickles and jams carefully into a newspaper. When she laid them on the kitchen counter, I felt rich again—look at the bounty! The pile of farm goods blessed those city counters. I touched each item, holding it, feeling its weight in my hand, smelling it. On the garlic was a trace of burlap from the bags in which it was stored. On the squash skin, sugar. On the carrots the dry breath of the walk-in cooler. And on the skin of the potatoes, I could smell the darkness of the soil, that beloved sandy loam. For a farmer, Thanksgiving is like Easter and Christmas braided together. It's a day to celebrate the harvest but also to hold the promise of a new season's beginning. Holding the food, the squash, the heavy glass jars, I could almost feel sunlight and sweat.

Right after breakfast Sarah and I met in the kitchen. We'd been planning the meal for a month over the phone. I had an apron ready for her and we reviewed our notes, scribbled on a piece of notebook paper. While Sarah and I cooked, Nick and Jayden watched basketball on TV, sitting cross-legged on the carpet. The cat wove between them and then out into the kitchen to stand between our bare feet begging for scraps. Nick and Jayden would wander into the kitchen for more coffee and tell us that everything smelled good, grabbing a quick bite before settling back in front of the game. Jayden was talking more than I had seen him for months and my first thought was to wonder what kind of new drugs he was on. But I only saw him shake out his usual pills—prescribed pain medication from orange plastic bottles—not the illegal stuff, which he'd hidden away in a drawer. He didn't start drinking until the afternoon when Sarah and I burst open the first bottle of champagne, toasting the meal that was baking in the oven.

Each time I picked up an ingredient its story unraveled back to the farm. The full, curvaceous butternut squash represented the completion of a cycle that started, months ago, in the palm of my hand. In May I had cupped the big squash seeds while using my right fingers to pluck up each one and place it in a square cell of compost. I had worked alone in the greenhouse with a radio to keep me company. The temperature rose. I had taken off my shirt, wearing only a pink bikini as I carefully pressed each seed into its place and then sunk it deep into the compost mix until my finger was buried up to the first knuckle. With a permanent marker, I'd written the variety of squash as well as the date, and then wedged the plastic tag into each tray. I had watered them every morning until the seeds broke above the soil surface in that joyous arch that seems universal in living things. The winter squash had grown quickly and smelled at the hottest point of the day like ripe squash flesh.

A few weeks later I'd planted the butternut seedlings in neat rows. Afterward, as I collected empty plastic trays, rain broke from the clouds and sealed the plant's transition from greenhouse to field. The summer's heat had fueled the squash plants and they burst out, forming a blanket of leaves and vines. Bees filled the orange flowers, spreading dusty pollen from plant to plant. The vines had scratched my shins as I hoed between the rows. Then, secretly, under that thick canopy, small fruit expanded with each rainstorm and grew into hourglass butternut. As the plants brittled in late summer the fruit began to harden and darken until, by the time I left for Portland, they were tan and shining with a silver coating of natural sugars, drawn out through the rind by the cooling nights.

Sarah and I skinned the squash and then cubed the bright orange flesh. We tossed them in olive oil and dusted them with sea salt and cinnamon. Our hands were sticky with sugar. Our cheeks were red from the heat in the kitchen, almost as they'd be at the farm, flushed from frost or the warm breath of a greenhouse. Sarah was smiling at me from a picture on the wall near the coffee pot and she was smiling at me from a few feet away from where she was chopping garlic. I looked back and forth, back and forth.

Peeling potatoes, I remembered the morning that Sarah and I had planted them. Nick had driven the tractor while Sarah and I rode behind on a set of raised chairs. A spiked wheel rolled along in front of us, carving marks a foot apart in the base of a trench, dug by blade mounted under the belly of the tractor. We dropped one potato on each mark, racing each other, yelling over the engine noise at Nick to speed it up until work became a game and we were tossing potatoes. After the trench was filled in, the white potato eyes grew stems underground and reached to the light while roots sprouted and dug deep into the soil.

We boiled the potatoes on the stove with salt until they were fork tender then drained them and mashed them with butter and milk. Jayden and Nick poured champagne into coffee cups and went out to the porch to smoke. Sarah and I watched their backs as we chopped vegetables. Nick's shoulders were broad from farm work, and he had neatly tucked his flannel shirt into a new pair of Carhartts. Jayden's slender form was hidden in the pajama pants and soccer jersey that had become his de facto uniform after dropping out of college. He refused to wear shoes and had been asked to leave the grocery store as we were shopping for Thanksgiving ingredients. I hadn't told Nick and Sarah about that. On the drive from the airport, I'd mentioned that he was recovering from a back injury and hadn't been able to keep up with his classes. They'd nodded respectfully and I noticed how gentle Nick was when he slapped him on the back, how lightly Sarah had shaken his hand. He was sick, I thought. Injured. But he was doing so well to cover it. I wondered if it hurt him or if he too was enjoying my friends' glow. He drank more and more and his cheeks flushed sweetly. I caught myself looking at him, drawn, as I had been for years, by his charm. It was easier than I'd expected, pretending that everything was okay. Jayden and I both faking this reunion just for the weekend but I wondered, in a brief flare, if maybe it would stick.

I cooked a small, locally raised turkey and made a pie from cherries harvested in an orchard outside the city. Sarah rolled the dough out with the rolling pin I bought a few days before. She rubbed it first with vegetable oil, seasoning the wood, she said. The turkey had been brined overnight in the fridge and it cooked quickly, browning to a caramel shine. The apartment smelled delicious. Nick and Jayden left their game and came to watch us, topping off their champagne glasses. Their elbows rested on the countertop bar. Nick, to one side, was handsome like a man in a movie from the 1940s, proportioned in that old-fashioned way, his chin blond with stubble, his blue eyes smiling through an early crinkle of crow's feet. Jayden looked soft and boyish, his curls swept to one side, rolling down his neck in dark loops, his eyes bright as a cat's. Maybe Nick was wearing off on him, I thought, as the two of them talked about the game. Nick's strength was contagious. But Jayden kept drinking. His face was flushing from pink to red and he'd begun, by the time the turkey was out of the oven, to dip forward into the swoop of his spine.

When Sarah and I were done cooking we set the dishes out on the counter: sweet potatoes, mashed russets, glazed carrots with roasted garlic, sweet pickles, red beet relish, bread stuffing with yellow onions from the farm, the small, browned bird, and a cherry pie, cooling on the balcony. We washed our hands. We hugged each other and we both smelled like the kitchen. I pressed my nose into her short blond hair and thought of all the hours I'd spent close to her in the barn, in the truck, in the hot air of the greenhouse, naked in the cold dark water of the river, sprawled like angels on the grass, crawling on hands and knees through a world of weeds. She felt real, heavy in my arms. I felt awake for the first time in months.

"Come on, come on," Nick scolded and we broke our embrace. He grabbed his camera and posed us, leaning over the feast, our cheeks rosy from the kitchen's heat, our hands stuffed in the pockets of dirty aprons. He stood back to take the picture. Jayden was behind him, his hands on his hips, happy drunk, grinning. It was the first time either of us had prepared Thanksgiving, and we were proud, presenting each dish to Jayden and Nick like gourmet chefs using terms like *caramelized* and *brined*.

We all stacked our plates high with the feast. Each cut into the vegetables was a return to the farm. "Remember," I'd say, and we'd break into a story. Jayden grew darker at each telling, excluded from our narrative. I watched him drift out slowly to that place where he'd been marooned since the summer. His lips pressed together tightly and his eyes grew hot from the pain. I studied him like I studied thunderclouds, trying to judge how close he was to breaking. I handed him a plate of turkey surrounded by vegetables and a freshly risen bun and he reached for butter and cranberry sauce with hunger, which I found promising. Maybe he'd make it through the meal. My pulse quickened, I could feel my eyes zipping from side to side, calculating his every move, trying to prevent our mask from slipping.

We sat in a circle on the king-sized bed since we didn't have a table in the apartment, balancing our plates in our laps. The mattress sagged slightly under our weight and we all tipped forward, drawn to an invisible point between us. Suddenly the apartment was very warm and close. The city became as silent as the farm on a late fall morning. We reached out for each other's hands and rested them on our knees. Altogether, without saying a word, we bowed our heads in silence.

I thought of a line from the Bible. It was meant to be a curse, but I said it as a prayer: "By the sweat of your brow you will eat your food until you return to the ground, since from it you were taken; for dust you are and to dust you will return."

We nodded *amen* and slowly opened our eyes, lifting them over the circle into the gaze of a neighbor. I was across from Sarah and caught her deep blue smiling stare and I jumped into it willingly. Nick and Jayden glanced at each other and I wondered what they saw. Nick's honest, strong eyes, his unflinching gaze, and Jayden's green irises, twisted by pain. They shook their heads like they were trying to break free. Nick turned to Sarah and me, smiling.

"Thank you for cooking," Nick said, and we let go of each other's hands and started to eat. Forking up great cubes of squash and potato, dipping turkey in gravy and wiping up the drippings with Sarah's soft, fresh bread, eating like eating was the answer to everything. It felt good to have such a simple need. To be so hungry. To have worked hard to realize something and to share in that with friends. We ate in silence and the city was silent too. The only sound was the sound of utensils on ceramic, champagne fizzing in mugs and the cat purring, wrapped up next to us.

After a second helping and huge slices of pie, covered in hand-whipped cream, the storm started to break.

Jayden went out to the porch for another cigarette. It was dim already, dusk falling quickly from the clouds that had rolled in after the morning's clearing which had revealed the mountain to us. He rested his elbows on the railing and I couldn't help but worry that he would jump. He smoked one, then another, and then he sat down at the patio table and hung his head back, gazing up to the sky. It began to drizzle. The cold, bone-aching rain of Oregon's winter. The rain first dusted his face and hair with little droplets then began to spread and soak. His T-shirt clung to his skin, pressing against his ribs and collar bones.

Nick was washing the dishes, his duty, he claimed, after all the work Sarah and I had done in earlier in the kitchen. His back was to the porch and to Jayden but Sarah, sitting with me on the bed, saw him. We were flipping through a magazine, gossiping, revisiting stories from the summer, making each other grin and blush.

"Is he OK?" she asked quietly, bowing her head to me. She looked out the glass door. Jayden was as unmoving as a corpse. We could feel the chill set in and knew how cold that rain felt on his skin. "Should we get him?" Her voice was worried.

I glanced at Jayden. "I'll go," I said.

I unfolded from the bed and slipped the glass door open. The porch wood was shockingly cool on my bare feet. A blast of damp air hit me across the face. "Jayden, you should come in." He didn't say anything. "You'll get sick out here." He shifted his crossed legs but didn't open his eyes. "Please."

"You're embarrassed by me," he whispered, slurred and bitter.

"No," I said quickly, "I just don't want them to worry about you. Sarah's worried."

"They feel bad for me."

"They're worried, that's all. I told them about your back." I opened the door a bit more and squeezed out onto the porch. The air was damp and shivering. I wrapped my arms around my chest. "Come in and watch some more TV with Nick." Jayden sat still. I thought for a moment, trying to come up with anything to get in him inside, out of the rain. Anything to make us look normal. To keep it up for just a few more days. "There's a bottle of whiskey. We'll make whiskeys and cider."

One limb at a time Jayden rose from the chair, slowly, as if every movement hurt. His curls dripped over his eyes. He stood and paused, steadying himself on the porch railing. He opened his eyes and they were his pain eyes, his blank, wet eyes, and I knew that there was no moving forward from this weekend, that it wasn't a new start but rather just another part of the same story. The story of his decline. Of our breaking. He didn't look at me as he shouldered past into the living room, shutting the door behind him so that I was stuck outside in the rain. The city was washed with lights in the fog. Clouds clung to the valley floor, flooding along the river. Each drop burned into my hot skin and I smelled the kitchen smoke and sugar wash from me. All the joy of our feast scrubbed away. Inside Sarah was rushing to get Jayden a towel and Nick's strong back still bent above the sink. I could hear dishes rattling and Sarah's soothing voice, but it wasn't a fix. It was just a temporary relief.

The next morning, I walked with Sarah down to the grocery store for more eggs to fix breakfast. Jayden and Nick were still sleeping off their hangovers. The light was soft, feathered through low clouds. We walked in silence under the dripping evergreens until we entered the cool breath of a tunnel, which wove under a roadway. Lit from overhead lights, it felt sheltered from the press of green and wet around us. In the middle of the tunnel, where our voices softly echoed off the cement, I paused. Our breath rose like fog.

"Jayden's messed up," I said, looking at my boots.

Sarah stood close to me, whispering, "I can tell."

"We're not together anymore." How could my heart break more for saying it? How could there be anything else left to shatter? I took a deep breath but my eyes were already stinging with tears. I was ashamed as much as I was hurt. I'd failed, I thought, to fix us. "He's dropped out of school. I don't know what to do."

"Is he like he was last night? All the time?" Sarah's eyes were huge with worry. I didn't want to share the pain with her, I didn't want her to leave burdened.

"Yes. Sometimes worse. He's taking tons of pills. Drinking all the time."

Sarah looked down and then up at me with the full force of her blue eyes. "He needs help. Can his mom come to get him? It's not your job to care for him."

I hadn't expected such ferocity from Sarah, who once nursed an injured pigeon back to life in a shoebox, who cried when rows were tilled under, who wept for diseased plants and refused to join us on woodchuck hunts. I'd thought she'd tell me to stay and make him better, to simply tend more dutifully, to share more love. Maybe she'd seen that I was bled out. I had nothing to give. The weight on my back had returned, heavy, drawing my shoulders low, and unlike a big bucket of weeds, holding that weight didn't make me stronger. Instead, it weakened me. I softened my lungs with a deep sigh and wiped the tears from my cheeks. They were cold on my skin and I could taste their salt.

"I feel like it is my job. He's my friend at least. He needs me." My voice was small and high, like a little girl's.

"Do you still love him?" Sarah whispered, reaching for my hand. Her palm was warm. She pressed my fingers together between hers and I could feel how strong her hands were, how much power she maintained from the season at the farm where she'd harvested and hauled and prepared the land for the spring. Her fingers were tough. Mine were soft and thin.

"I don't know," I said. "Not like I used to. But I want to make him better."

Sarah nodded. She understood, as a farm girl, the desire to heal. "I get it."

"I'd hoped he wouldn't act up, you know, while you guys were in town. I just wanted us to have a good time." I kicked my boots in the mossy path. There was something so devastating about this transparency. It had been much easier to pretend that everything was alright.

"Don't worry about us!" Sarah said, taking my hand and leading me forward, out of the tunnel and into the dim light of morning. "We're so happy to be out here. It's nearly winter at the farm, you know," she added. "Everything is packed up and put to sleep for the season. There isn't much to do there right now."

We walked the last few blocks to the grocery store giggling about how nervous Nick had been on the flight and about how he liked to take us out in the truck when the fields were empty and muddy to spin out in donuts, the two of us pressed together in the cab by the force of the truck's spinning, laughing so loudly that we drowned out the country music on the radio. We traveled back to the farm all weekend and even though it was cold there at the time, in our memories it was summer and sweetly hot. We sweated and the sun burned our skin and our hands were dirty, our feet wet. Even as we drove out to the ocean, or wandered the bookstores downtown, or sipped tea in the Japanese Gardens, we weren't really in Portland. We were back at Cedar Circle.

Jayden lingered like a ghost at the edge of our conversation, blurred by pain and pills, and quieted by our laughter. He drifted further and further away as the weekend came to a close, repelled, I felt, by how bright I was growing in their company. My limbs felt stronger. My cheeks ached from smiling. I looked like the girl he'd chosen to leave behind. The girl he'd planned to be unfaithful to in the summer while she faithfully tended to the fields. I saw it in the way he looked at me. I was an affront to him, somehow offensive in my vitality. I slept so far away from him in bed that I woke one morning with one of my feet on the floor. I could have flown back with them forever. I dreamed of it—escaping back to the farm in November—but the more I thought of it the more I imagined Jayden, alone in the apartment, left to tear through what remained of his life, and I became ashamed and burdened and heavy again in my bones.

On our last night in the city we drank downtown at a pub and coming back to the apartment through the wash of lights on the freeway I felt that there was a chance, for all of us, to be where we wanted to be. I sensed that I was returning to something that I alone was tasked with, just like, at the farm, I was tasked with seeding, or attending the farmers market. I let that sense of need brighten my future. I let it seep into the evening. As I hugged Sarah goodnight and heard the door on the guest bedroom click shut, I hoped that what I'd gained in their presence would stick with me. The strength to continue. I'd come back to them one day soon, I knew it.

My place, for this season, was in Portland. I looked across the sea of the bed at Jayden's face in the light of the city. His eyes were shut and he could have been dead, he was laying so still. His face was very white and his lips were opened slightly as if he might whisper a poem to the ceiling. He'd crossed his hands over his chest and in every way, he looked like the boy I had once loved. But the harder I looked the less love I could raise for him in my heart. I stared at him until he was flat. Until I felt nothing at all. Until he was a specter.

In the fall, nothing grows, creating no futures, only the chores of putting things to rest. It is an undertaker's season. The work list includes pulling up the trellises that once supported peas and peppers, ripping up plastic that protected melons and cucumbers from spreading weeds, oiling the tools and parking the trucks and tractors in their winter lots. The earth is tilled and made bare again. When the plow comes through it flips the surface upside down. Roots and dead leaves are hidden, their memories are erased. In the fall the crew works in silence, people hold their tongues like they are in a graveyard. The gunshots of goose hunters echo across the valley so loud I wince each time.

For a week it rains. One by one I clean the onions and box them up. When the greenhouse is empty, I sweep up their scattered skins. The garlic is sorted and the slings are hung back in the corner of the barn where they will wait until next August. Winter squash is polished, one fruit at a time, with a cotton rag then nestled against each other in crates. When I finish packing a crate, I add it to a stack on the first floor of the barn. The crates are so heavy that the floor warps and slips back into the foundation.

In the rain, everyone is as withdrawn as I am and I feel no pressure to smile. I go back deep into my head. Into countries of memory and sunlight. I try to go forward too, daydreaming about other futures, but all I see are seasons. The dull stone of fall will freeze and the world will be purified by the cold. Then a break in the ice, and spring will stream up from underground and summer will burst forth, green and busy with the sky huge and hot overhead. The farm's future gives me one too. I don't know if I will survive that winter without the promise of work, of dirty hands and sprouting seeds, just like the garlic and berries need straw mulch to protect them.

I imagine years ticking away like that, season by season: the light greens of spring, the jeweled fruit of summer, the dark, earthy flavors of fall. As a farm girl I am needed, I tend to the cycles; I am an attendant to the patterns of the land. In the future, I don't see myself, just the crops, in neat rows and tall hedges. I see boxes of freshly picked tomatoes and quarts of heaped berries like other girls see homes and cars and well-set tables.

By the end of the week of rain, I find myself in the barn, where all our stories start. In the barn, the idea of being devoted to the fields is universal. Here, men have spent their lives. Here, animals rested after plowing up the rich soil. I can touch the oiled posts and beams and know that I am not alone. With the rain high above on the roof, the barn is muted and dark. The stone foundation holds the chill of early fall nights and it rises up through the floorboards. The big sliding doors frame the wet driveway and the limp basketball hoop. The farm stand, soaked with mud, hunches near the closed-up greenhouses and the dark picnic tables, all of its terracotta pots stacked and stored for the winter. Bright orange pumpkins line the retail tables, glistening in the rain. Itchi lies curled up in the forgotten sweatshirt of some summer crew member, wrapped in a perfect, grey circle. When I pet him, he doesn't stir. This is sleeping weather. Weather in which to gain strength for the cold to come.

I tell myself I will go home when I am done cleaning the tools. There I will shower the cold out of my bones and make myself a cup of herbal tea. But then there will be nothing but the bed. The cat will sit in the window, watching the birds flit through the rain and I will watch her and think about drawing her, but I won't. I won't do anything.

At the farm I keep busy. I am the last to leave at the end of the day, as if I can't stand to say goodbye. I do all the little chores that no one else finds the time for, cleaning the trucks, sweeping the barn. Before the real cold sets in I want to oil the hand tools so that their steel will shine all winter and no rust will flower on their blades. I take every hoe off the tool rack and lay their sharp edges across my lap. I can't help but think of all the hands that have touched the polished wood handles: Hannah, white-blond in the summer light; Charlie, who always made me laugh; James, barefoot in running shorts.

One at a time I brush a rag soaked with vegetable oil over the blades, and then set the hoes back up on their hooks. They have saved the pumpkins from drowning in a sea of weeds, cleaned up the new strawberry fields, been leaned on at the end of a row, looking back over the planting toward to the river. Their blades are razor-sharp, perfected by whetstones that we carry in our back pockets. Their handles are shapely ash, rounded at the base and I lay each to rest for the winter kindly, like tucking in a child.

I imagine the world waking in spring and a shaft of light breaking through a sliver in the barn boards flashing off the slick blades of the hoes, fresh and ready to cut the wet soil. My heart quickens at the thought of growing.

Then I clean the shovels and the hand hoes, the trowels, the lips of the posthole digger, the harvesting knives, the scissors, and the stirrup hoes. I even wipe down the blade of the sickle that hangs above our tools, huge and ominous like a cruel smile, a relic of harder days. My hands are slick with oil and my rag is stained dark with dirt and rust. Finally the tools hang in their hooks, well ordered, ready for a new year. All the memories and grit have been washed from them.

I sit on the edge of the stairs and listen. Rain drips down from the roof. Underground, little things settle; there is always a sense of movement in the barn, except in deep winter when everything is frozen. On the road, a car swishes past but doesn't stop at the farm stand. Rain on the maple leaves. Rain on the hard-skinned pumpkins. Rain on the roof of Yoda and the other farm truck. The coolers' motors rumbling, clicking off every few minutes and then real silence before they begin again. I am exactly where I want to be, I think, and totally alone.

CHAPTER THIRTEEN

One night I sat at the kitchen counter, bending over my textbooks. I closed my ears while Jayden turned up the drooping voice of a sports announcer on the TV. He'd narrowed his interests to poetry, drugs, and basketball; the only thing that would draw him out of the back room was more booze or an NBA game. He would have moved the TV back there if it hadn't been so heavy. In the living room Jayden lay on his stomach, like a child in front of the game, as the Lakers filled the screen with purple and yellow flashes.

Focus, I repeated to myself, flipping through my textbooks, trying to land on a word that made sense, but the lines just bled through my head. I was still an A-grade student but the work was harder to fit in. My eyes were often heavy and my reading felt endless. *Focus*.

I slammed my book shut at the heaving sound of Jayden vomiting up his gin.

"Fuck!" I said, jumping off my barstool to grab a towel in the kitchen, too disgusted to look at him. When I came back to clean up his mess, he had scraped the white bile back into his tumbler.

Then he tilted the glass back and drank it.

My stomach rolled and rose in my throat. "What the hell are you doing?" I yelled.

"It's mostly gin," he said, shrugging. He'd emptied the bottle and knew that I had stolen his keys so he couldn't drive out to get another. So, instead of getting a little less drunk, he'd decided to drink his vomit off the carpet, swallowing the cup of puke before I could snatch it away.

I sprayed the stain with foam cleaner and dabbed at it with a paper towel. Jayden had already drifted off into the dark green room, ashamed or uncaring, I couldn't tell.

My exhaustion had turned to disgust. *He drank his vomit off the carpet*, I wrote to his mother in an email. *I am really worried about him.*

And I'm afraid I'll come home and he'll be dead. But I didn't write that. I shut my laptop and turned off the light.

Later that week Jayden tripped on the vacuum cleaner while he wandered around in the dark in the middle of the night. It roared to life and he started screaming. I woke up terrified that someone had broken into our apartment. It took all my courage to switch on the bedside lamp and then I saw him, standing by the vacuum cleaner, his hands wringing out his curls, his eyes glassy from drugs, crying as the machine sucked on one spot of carpet.

In Portland early winter was overcast and wet, the sky a low, soft ceiling that drew horizons in. It rained every day. My shoes never dried out; they were still damp from yesterday's puddles when I laced them on in the morning.

Black mold blossomed along the trim-board in the bath-room. Jayden and I stopped speaking. He shuffled and slammed doors. I stomped around and clattered the plates in the dishwasher while I knew he was sleeping. If I needed to see if he was alive, I would shake the pills in the junk drawer where he kept a collection of orange prescription bottles and he'd appear, like a trained dog, afraid that I was throwing them out. I carried the weight of his living or dying like a backpack full of stones.

In the weeks before Christmas break, I emailed his mother again and begged her to keep him home for the rest of the school year. I had to make her understand that his behavior wasn't creative or experimental, but rather potentially fatal. But she'd lived for decades on a schedule similar to Jayden's addict life, sleeping through the day and crashing around the house at night, leaving at 2:00 A.M. go grocery shopping, and napping through the afternoon. She hid cash, drugs, and cases of champagne in her painting studio and would whip them out to celebrate full moons, tennis championships, or her Chihuahuas' birthdays. Living with her was like being in a never-ending surprise party. She resembled a furious Stevie Nicks, swathed in gypsy shawls, UGG boots, and John Lennon glasses and I was equal parts in love with her and terrified of her volcanic personality.

Please, I should I have written, *I can't do this anymore. I'm fading away. Please. I can't be held responsible.*

By the end of the month I wanted to walk out of the apartment and never return. I also dreamed of filling with resolve and finally bringing Jayden back around, like a goddess diverting a river with her palm. I wanted to tell everyone he had disappeared so our memories could remain unblemished: our hands sailing over the spines of books in dusty stores, the night he had seen fireflies dancing for the first time in the field behind my parents' house, the sunset on a black beach in northern California when we carved our names into a driftwood trunk, connected like an equation, with a plus sign. As other apartments started to hang Christmas lights on their porches or in their windows, I made him go for walks with me through the wet neighborhoods, stepping over the cracks and puddles. I tried every day to make him better but I was becoming bitter towards him and doubted that recovery was possible. He used up all the love I had leftover. I played his friend then his mother, then his nurse, then nothing at all.

The fields are dark and hard under the sky. We have parked the trucks and tractors neatly, rolled down the sides of the hoop houses, latched the greenhouse doors against winter gale storms and pruned the blueberries so that they are bare arms scratching at the clouds. Right now, the farm is in a death-like sleep, like Juliet after drinking Friar Laurence's poison. Dead but living.

By the sweat of your brow, you will eat your food until you return to the ground since from it you were taken; for dust you are and to dust, you will return. I think it is so beautiful, this cycle from dust to dust. As a farm girl, I need to see where I will return when my work is done. I understand sweat on my face and eating the food that I raise from the soil. Although I sow the seeds and hoe the earth and take what fruit I want from the lush plantings I, too, am dust, destined to be ground back into the dirt when I die, just like the corn, or strawberries, or kale plants. Everything back into that one ocean of chemistry, all one and the same.

What would I miss if I was forever in the ground? I wonder.

I close my eyes and immediately it comes to me: The smell of wet soil. The feel of the silty road under my bare feet. The tight pull of a sunburn on my back. The first strawberry, still hard, just barely flushed red but still sweeter than I could imagine. A drift of honey locust blossoms on the edge of the road like June snow. A patch grown over in a sea of pumpkin vines. Sweet corn sugar on my cheeks. A clean field. The shaft of my hoe wet with sweat. Dipping my tongue into the glass neck of a Corona to search out a lime's bitterness. A pattern of red and green lettuces stretching hundreds of feet into the distance. Rain falling on the waxy leaves of cabbage. An heirloom tomato like the heart of some magical creature, veined in yellow and green. Standing with Luke and Nick at the end of the day and watching a summer rainstorm wash the farm clean. Staying late as the shadows fade into the night, the spring stars crisp above the shapes of the hills.

I read back through my favorite books, searching for a text to describe my journey, but find nothing. I don't have the words myself to say what I learn at the farm and how it has formed a holy book. Its words are written on the land, in a language older than anything living, composed of stardust, comet ice, hydrogen combustion and the smoothing pressure of time. Under weather, under seasons and cycles, lay patterns that, through a farm girl's constant study, become scripture; a Bible, Veda or Koran. In them, I find the way to live, to be good, to be part of something connected and graceful. I could name those things *gods* or *spirits*, but I imagine them as one bigger motion, a wheel. It turns water to rain, to mist, to snow, to cloud and over and over again forever.

Being a farm girl keeps me alive. It's my lifeline, something to wake for, always another season, another year, another long day. It doesn't patch me up entirely but it allows me to move forward, one crawling, creeping month at a time through winter until spring breaks. I turn myself, molecule by molecule, into part of the farm.

CHAPTER FOURTEEN

I returned to New Hampshire in the darkness of a winter day that stretched across the continent. Clouds covered the land all the way from Portland to the East Coast. I lay my cheek on the cold window of the plane and let its engines rattle me to the bone. At the airport Mom brought me dinner to eat on the ride north and I noticed the familiar taste, her seasoning the way it had always been. I was startled because in the few months I had been gone I felt that everything had changed but it was, I realized, just me who was altered, thin and ghostly.

Colored lights drew us down the driveway, hung on metal posts that Dad pounded into the ground before it froze solid for the year. They looked like the handholds of a rope bridge, guiding the car into the garage. The lights cast shadows on the snow, forming little pools under each bulb, shimmering gold or bright pink, green and blue.

I helped Mom drag my suitcase out of the backseat and up the steps into the kitchen. For a second I stopped there, wiping my feet on the rough mat, struck by the smell. Every part of it was the same. The smell of home was a complex perfume and I could pick out each thread— clementine rinds, the blue spruce Christmas tree needles, maple logs on the fire, the musk of the humidifier pumping fog by the piano in the music room, the tang of the Carmex which we all smeared on our cold bitten lips, the dog and cat hair roasting in the grates of the heaters behind the old couches that deep in their bones would always smell like popcorn and cough syrup from the sick days we spent sleeping on them.

I knew Mom had cleaned and reorganized before she picked me up, always nervous that we'd come back to a messy home, but that didn't change a thing. My sister Elise lay on the couch she always preferred, her feet up on a pillow, her old white cat Princess shaking its tail. Hannah rested belly-down on the rug in the middle of the room, while my brother rocked in the rocking chair. Even though I couldn't see him, I knew Dad was in the kitchen, washing dishes, afraid that Mom would come home and catch him relaxing while there was housework to be done. For a second I caught them all where they rested and the sameness made me feel small, then comfortable, then lost again as they all sprung up and came to me, my dog jumping to land a kiss on my cheek.

Dragging my suitcase upstairs I passed the photo collages that filled our halls. The frames progressed from right to left, starting at the door by my parents' bedroom where the pictures showed their first house outside of Boston, my mom's big 80s hair and my dad's short shorts.

One by one the kids appeared as naked babies, then naked kids in the bathtub. We went apple picking, we dressed up for Halloween, we opened presents or stood on the bald tops of New England mountains by summit signs; we were cute, then awkward, then half grown-up.

Walking along with them, pulling my heavy rolling suitcase, I became quickly embarrassed to see myself in braces, then wearing kimonos and yellow-tinted glasses to school while Elise grew slim and strutted around in crop tops and skin-tight capris that showed a slice of her neon thong. By the time I reached the carpeted stairs that led to my bedroom, I was fully aware of my place in the family.

"Megan's the artistic one," Mom would explain to her friends or the meat guy at the grocery store who she's known long enough from her weekly shopping trips to consider a friend. "We just don't know where she came from!"

I had always been more outside than inside my family, drawn to the woods and fields more than the comforts of the home. From the first steps to my bedroom, before they turned a corner and headed up to the third-floor hallway, I looked down and saw our Christmas tree from above. Our Christmas trees always sat in the same corner of the living room so in peering down there was a sense of timelessness in the space; Christmas when I was five, ten or fifteen looked just the same. Our childhood ornaments—crafted from Popsicle sticks and cotton balls—cluttered the sharp needles. On the top, an angel rested, tilting a bit forward, her skirts glowing with pulsing light. The angel seemed half asleep as she smiled down on us.

I put my bag away and then slipped downstairs to join in the flood of warmth and conversation. The living room filled with heat from the wood fire. Hannah, Jake, Elise and I lay on the carpet, playing board games marked by our childhood: Monopoly with handwritten property cards, Sorry with Lego men standing in for lost pieces, Battleship with plastic fleets damaged by the teeth of a puppy who was now the old dog sleeping by the fire.

That first night home quickly turned stormy outside. I could hear the town plows scraping along the frozen ground and the sifting sound as the trucks dropped salt up the neighborhood roads, but inside the living room blazed, the fire snapping and eating through logs. I felt that I knew myself there like I knew the land. I could chart it in my dream space—the blue house, the road along the river, the bridge, and then the graceful smoothness of the farm's fields, its hedgerow trees, the barn's anchoring redness, heart-like in the center of it all. I went to bed with the sense of being embraced.

In the morning I heard the farm softly calling, a whisper smothered by snow. It sounded different in December, a quiet voice, buried deep under hard soil. The waters froze and the trees lost their rippling leaves, even the oaks were naked by December. The little animals that ran through all the warm days—through the barn rafters, through the soil—slept in their deep hollows underground. Birds, whose shadows and songs swept through the fields, had flown south. Only the chickadees

remained, repeating their names to each other desper-
ately, huddled in the branches of the bare apple trees,
where the last fruit hung withered and browned.

On the day of the winter solstice I drove to the farm,
making my way slowly across the green metal bridge so
I could savor that familiar sweep in the river's turning.
The day dimmed as the sky filled with grey storm clouds.
The windows in The Yellow House were dark, and I knew
that Will and Kate weren't home. I had hoped to see Nick
and Luke but they had gone somewhere too. I could see
in the driveway where their trucks had backed up earlier
that morning. Itchi the cat didn't hibernate but he slept
long through the day in secret hiding places. His tracks
led from his food bowl to the barn and out to the shed.
He wouldn't come running even if I called.

I walked past the farm stand, through the center
of the barn and followed a snowshoe trail out into the
fields. Snow lay flat and white on the acres, reducing
the landscape to abstract geometric shapes. Black trees.
White fields. Grey sky. The silence in winter, in its true
December center, sounded like a hibernating heartbeat, a
pulse so low that I almost thought I dreamed it. In winter
memories of movement ghosted through me but the
fields were frozen solid. Only memory made the land rise
again, but no matter how vivid the image it just quivered,
like snow falling from pine boughs. I felt erased by the
stillness of it.

I tried to imagine movement in the still fields, the
running shadow of a rain cloud, sprinkler heads rotating, clicking like a clock's hand, sweat running down my

backbone, between my breasts, into my ears and eyes. I struggled to picture all the colors: the blue-green of leek leaves, the red of ruby cabbage, how orange the pumpkins ripened under their grey-green canopy, the black raspberry stains that took days leaving my fingertips. The farm came back to life in memory and I could feel the rush of wind through the truck window as I sped down the road to harvest. I could see the wavering heat of July rippling along the edges of the fields. I watched as storms pushed back the rigid trees in great gusts and tore off leaves, reshaping the dirt roads with flooding water. I saw myself walking the rows again, end to end, harvesting carrot bunches, pulling weeds, lying in the shade, crashing into the river at the end of the day—a cannonball of a girl, exploding through the water. The summer's pulse ran under December's cold, like water beneath ice.

I followed the snowshoe trail down through the center of the fields to the river. The cabin sat empty. The dock had been pulled up and lay buried in snow. Beyond the banks the river had become a flat white road, crossed by animal prints, connecting Vermont to its neighboring state. Snow filled the chairs by the fire pit, resting on the seats and along the arms.

It had been several months since I'd sat around that fire, watching sparks meet stars. The river was always a place of celebration. We ran to it to cool off, marking the ends of hard days or dragging in the irrigation pipe at the start of the season. We drew water from the river with aluminum irrigation pipes. A rusty old tractor sat on the bank all season, unable to drive anymore. Its only job was to power the pump. When it ran it rattled the dock and made so much noise that we had to yell over the roaring diesel engine. The river saved crops from drought; it fattened melons and zucchini, cooled lettuce heads in July heat, and protected strawberry blossoms from late frosts. But in December the river was just a flattened path of snow.

On these banks, many summers ago, I lingered into the afternoon with Cyrus. He was on the field crew too and I liked his name—Cyrus Birch—and his green eyes. Work in the fields had been canceled for the afternoon because the National Weather Service forecasted a huge thunderstorm, crashing through the western hills of Vermont, set to roll over the farm sometime after lunch. The dam south of us had been let out in preparation for the coming deluge, leaving the riverbanks exposed; they rose out of the water, silty slick and littered with drift-wood skeletons and tires. Excited by the storm and the freedom of the afternoon, Cyrus and I had crawled up the bank until we reached the green metal bridge.

"Come on," he'd said, and took my hand out to the middle of its span. We stepped onto the railing and held onto the riveted crossbeams. Below us, the river ran deep and brown, maybe 75 feet down, far enough that my stomach wobbled and caught in my throat. I was afraid of jumping but more afraid to say no.

We counted 1-2-3 and held hands as we jumped until we hit the water and broke apart. My legs were in a straight pike and I went so far down I worried I would hit the bottom. But I rose and came up full of sparks.

Drenched and grinning we took the muddy banks back to the farm, every inch of our bodies covered in silt. I spat out mud tasting like primal ingredients—the recipe for life: water, soil, blood metal rust, starlight mica chips, fishbone splinters. We crawled up near the dock between the two spruce trees. As the storm broke, we held out our arms and the rain fell on us in huge, warm drops. Mud ran down our bodies in little waterways, following the lowest points of our anatomy, right down our centers, over our legs and down to the earth. Like an animal, I was all touch and smell and sound. Washed clean, unburdened, I became a creature of elemental powers, not just a girl but something transformed, risen like the legend of the phoenix—not of fire, but of earth.

Everywhere I walked, even in the cold press of snow, I stepped over histories. Here, in June of that year, I had woken early by the riverbank, as the birds first started calling to each other. After the Strawberry Festival, the farm hosted a big dinner for staff and volunteers and it went on late into the next morning. We ate leftovers and potluck dishes and drank cases of warm beer. Someone always had a guitar and another person would open up and sing, or pull a set of drums from the bed of their truck. It had been particularly warm during that Festival and after a few beers the field crew, quickly drunk, ran down the dock naked and swam like seals in the dark river. Later, the crew fell asleep on the porch or in tents around the lawn, or in the beds of the farm trucks, or simply on the grass. I woke early in my tent to the faint flush of dawn and walked back to the fire pit.

Nick slept belly down, with his face near the coals. I
sat on a log looking at my friend. We had drunk hard the
night before. That morning's hangover seemed a cloudy
sort of separation from reality. I was groggy and my
hair smelled like wood smoke and cigarettes. Fog lifted
from the river's surface in great spiraling ribbons. The
world kept sleeping; there was just the two of us and the
songbirds. Nick picked himself up and dusted the ash off
his face and arms. There were unopened bottles of red
wine on the picnic table and he pulled out a cork and
drank from the green glass neck. We pretended, for an
hour, that we were homesteading together. We claimed
everything—our river, our fire, and our day out ahead of
us—for ourselves. We joked that we might really be alone
in the world and that we would have only what we saw
before us: fields, lawn, battered farm trucks, a cabin, our
thick hands, and dirty feet. Our lips stained with red wine,
we slipped off the end of the dock and into the warm
river, letting the current take us south until we drifted
past Cedar Circle and had to swim hard to get back to
the dock.

That memory seemed impossible in December, the
water now a solid sheet of white, the fields covered, flattened by the season, the acres throbbing with loneliness
between dark hedgerows. I walked back up through the
snowshoe tracks. Itchi didn't run out to see me. I looked
in a few of his hiding spots but I couldn't find him.

That night I returned for a holiday dinner at the
farm. Will and Kate liked to throw parties for their
friends and the few staff that remained at that time of

year. Will cooked elaborate Mexican feasts. Having grown up in the fields of Southern California, he learned from migrant workers and old Latino farm owners how to dice hot peppers and grind tortilla corn. Their kitchen brimmed with the thick brown scent of mole, the green spice of tomatillo sauce, the sweet singe of carrot habanero salsa, black bean chili darkness, lime bright ceviche bite. The table was draped in a multi-colored Mexican cloth and a painted ceramic cactus held flickering, blood-red candles. I put my plate of homemade sugar cookies on the counter and hugged the hosts. Will always wore a T-shirt and sweatpants no matter how formal the occasion. He had braided his long white hair into pigtails. When I hugged Kate, her beaded necklaces pressed against my neck and I noticed the touches of aromatherapy oils on her throat and wrists. Their smiles were like moonslivers.

We sat around the table. Nick, Sarah, and Luke were there, along with Luke's girlfriend and a dozen other people. We passed Kate's colorful collection of ceramic serving platters in a great circle, sampling organic tequilas out of rose-tinted shot glasses. Our faces blazed with the alcohol and body heat, from chilies and spices. Will made his sauces with the farm's tomatoes and peppers, canned or frozen in late summer. As we dipped into a salsa, he explained what tomatoes he had chosen, or how hot the jalapeños were that year because it had been dry. I sat across from a plate-glass window so I could see myself in the reflection. I remember the pink of my cheeks and the whites of everyone's smiles, a rainbow of bowls going round and round, hands reaching toward the red cactus candles to pour another shot of tequila. December in Vermont was a season of stillness, of deep cold, but we were transported to a summer climate, a night in August, thick with heat and the sounds of living things: night birds, voices from across the river, the crops swishing in a low breeze, a little wake lapping against the watergrass and lily pads. The landscape was levitated by memory.

CHAPTER FIFTEEN

I returned to my apartment in a steady rain that beat on the windshield and slushed under the tires. I didn't put on any music. Instead, I just listened to the rain and watched as the lights of the city's great bridges rose and receded. I couldn't quite believe I was back in Portland, but there was the neon glow of Old Town's Portland Oregon sign and the tall buildings in the Pearl District casting wet shimmers on the waters of the Willamette. I sank lower into my seat as I pulled into the parking lot and looked up at the windows on the third floor. I could see my cat pressed between the glass and the blinds. Throwing my backpack over my shoulder I hiked up the stairs, enjoying the loud thumps of my farm boots on the wet wood. They echoed viciously in the stairwell. I knocked on our front door but Jayden didn't come out of his room. I dug my key from a back pocket and let myself in.

"Hello!" I called. The place smelled of smoke and mold. When it rained hard, water dripped down the chimney and black spots spread like fuzzy dark flowers on the inside of the fireplace. I flicked on the lamp. The cat ran up to greet me, twining between my legs.

Near the kitchen, between the entryway and the living room, Jayden lay face down on the carpet. His arms and legs spread wide in broken angles. A dozen orange pill bottles were scattered around him. A bottle of wine had tipped over near his right hand and a blood-like stain pooled from its neck. An empty fifth of gin rested on its side, the clear glass shining in the lamplight. It looked like a scene from a movie, too staged to be real. At first, I was upset with Jayden for staining the carpet and for trying to make me feel bad about spending my holiday away from him. I thought it was a set up.

"Jayden," I called. "Come on, wake up."

I put my backpack and keys down. I didn't want to play into his drama. Instead, I fed the cat and filled her water dish.

"Jayden," I said, after putting the dish down on the kitchen floor. I poked his ribs with my toe. "Wake up."

His mouth hung open. White foamy spit was dried to his lips, dripping down to the carpet. I poked him again. "Jayden, seriously, this is ridiculous. Get up."

I tried to roll him over with my foot. His face was too white; his lips icy pale.

For months, I'd worried about coming home and finding him dead and now he lay there, just as I had pictured a hundred times. The thought was like jumping into freezing water. I stood over him and grabbed his shirt by the shoulders and shook him violently. Every part of my body felt electric.

"Wake up! Wake up!" I kept shaking him until his eyes rolled around in their sockets and opened slowly.

He squinted and licked his dry lips. "What are you doing back so early?" he asked, dazed.

I told him the date.

"No way," he muttered. "No way. It's Friday."

"It's Sunday. Do you need to go to the hospital?"

He shook his head back and forth in a slow *no*. I pulled him up so he sat against the wall, slumped like a doll. Quickly I rifled through the empty pantry, and made him a peanut butter and jelly sandwich. He ate it like he couldn't taste anything. I set a glass of water beside him and started picking up the orange prescription bottles.

"Did you take all my pills again?" he asked groggily, wiping the crumbs from the corner of his mouth.

"No," I said. "I've been gone for two weeks."

He sat there for an hour, watching TV through squinted eyes while I scrubbed the carpet. "Do you need to go to the hospital?" I asked again. I knew they wouldn't want to see him. He'd already been kicked out of the three closest emergency rooms for pill hunting.

"I'll just take a shower," he said.

I waited until I could hear the shower running before I called his mom. She picked up immediately and I could tell from her frantic breath that she knew why I was reaching out. Maybe she'd felt something shiver through her, some forecast of doom, or maybe his silence was what tipped her off. I stepped onto the cold porch to talk to her, keeping my voice low.

"I'm on my way," she said. Before we hung up she

asked me to keep him in the apartment, fearing that he might try to run if he knew that she was coming. When she presented the idea of treatment to him over Christmas break, he had said *fuck that, you'll never get me there alive.* So we planned to keep her visit a secret. She would call his dad—her ex—and they would fly up early Tuesday morning. The fact that the two of them would travel north together told me that she was taking this seriously. I'd never known them to share a car, or even a phone call, peacefully. The only thing I had to do was to keep Jayden distracted and alive until they got there.

That evening I emailed my professors and told them couldn't come to class on Monday, making some lie about my stomach being upset. Then I found Jayden's keys and put them in a pint of half-eaten, freezer-burnt ice cream. I took his wallet and tucked it under my bed.

After the adrenaline left me, after Jayden collapsed on the air mattress in the dark back room, after the cat relaxed and lay sleeping beside me, I realized my hands were shaking. The muscles in my throat quivered like twine before it snapped under too much weight. I turned off the light and told myself to stay on guard in case Jayden tried to leave during the night. I slept so lightly I woke each time a leaf blew across the porch, or a car drove through the neighborhood, or a plane flew high above the roof, off to brighter climates.

☘

The heart of the farm slows when the ground freezes solid and the river becomes a road of white. I can hear

Luke's hammer striking steel as I walk behind the pines to the row of hoop houses. The plastic skins hold beads of ice frost. Even the texture of the earth under my boots is different. The ground which I've tilled and opened is closed. I count and plan and clean in the cold breath of the barn, preparing for spring. Luke spends the warmest hours of the day constructing a back room to the big greenhouses where we grow tomatoes during the summer. He looks huge and stiff in his winter clothing and I hardly recognize his shape against the arched piles of plowed snow.

We sit inside the open structure with our backs up against the new wall as if it could offer some protection from the cold. I tuck my nose into my collar and stuff my hands deep in my pockets. We dream a common dream of warmth. It's a memory dream, a list of days we spent sweating in this same structure, working the soil as it breathed fresh in spring, planting tomato seedlings under the glare of the plastic, harvesting in heat that rose into the hundreds. It's a place of dizzy exhaustion and green tomato pollen but in the heart of winter, the air bites hard. To stay warm Luke builds the cabin for me with words—one measurement at a time—until he describes the whole space, the peaked roof above our heads, the two doors opening to the field along the road. We shiver in silence at this vision. This reformation.

January forms resolutions; the snow became a clean slate to draw and dream upon. Farming offers, always, a chance to recreate the world; to do it again, better. *Time to push the reset button,* we say to each other, circling back to the starting line. In the open frame at the back of the greenhouse, Luke and I talk about the things that will be: the heating system that will sit protected in the new structure, the early tomatoes that will grow there, warmed through the cold spring nights, their tight skins and soft flesh. Later I remember how we shivered, how the framing created enough of an idea to imagine a roof overhead. We believe we can do better, always.

Under the soil, under the frost line, a world which I can't see and can hardly imagine continues to spin and multiply. Stardust and microscopic creatures convert sunlight and nitrogen into the building blocks of creation. Even though the fields are blank they contain all of next year's potential, shimmering, right below the snowline. As the cold bites through our many layers of jackets, Luke and I imagine that it is summer and we are picking tomatoes in the greenhouse, our cheeks and fingers red from heat and green from plant pollen. Sweat runs like private rivers down our bodies and into our boot tops. We stomp our freezing feet on the hard ground, trying to drum up blood. Only dreams warm us in winter.

CHAPTER SIXTEEN

I started cleaning in the morning, moving each book off the shelf and wiping away the dust. I swept the pollen from the glass on the patio table. I scooped out the cat litter and washed each shelf in the fridge. I wanted the place clean, like the sky after a rainstorm. The sun rose directly behind Mount Hood, its sharp peak a black menace on the horizon before light broke over it and spilled down the valley. It hit against windowpanes and windshields, sparking through the city.

When Jayden shuffled to the bathroom, I told him I wasn't going to class, that my stomach was upset. He said nothing. I heard him turn on the shower and stand under it so long I knew that the water had turned cold.

That morning his mom emailed me her flight plans. She and her ex would come in early the next day, rent a car and be at the apartment before noon. At the end of her message she thanked me for things I didn't feel I deserved. After all, I had left him to overdose, I had waited too long to call, I had given up. Hours crept by like shadows. I watched as they crossed the carpet, imagining the coming silence when the apartment would be mine entirely and the silence would be like snow in my mind.

Jayden noticed something strange near dinnertime. Maybe I was too quiet. Maybe he could sense my nervousness. I often forgot that he'd known me for four years. The drugs might have changed the boy I knew but they hadn't altered my behavior or our history.

"What's happening?" he begged me.

I kept my face straight until I couldn't any longer. My excitement over his departure weakened my lie. He pressed me for answers until I confessed. All the tension left his body when the words spilled out of my lips. He sat down limply on the barstool next to me, where we used to eat dinner, reading poetry books, sharing lines with each other like other couples might exchange bites of food.

"Okay," he said. "I understand."

Then he began crying and did not stop until after midnight. He pleaded with me through sobs that choked him so badly I was afraid that he would drown, he begged to spend the night with me in the big bed in the living room.

"One last time," he said. "Please."

I thought of it as a vigil. I would keep him safe. It was the only way I could imagine sleeping with him. I let him lay beside me even though his touch repulsed me. I drew away from him as he curled around me, his tears soaking into my hair. I turned and he rolled onto his side and I surrounded him. I made myself pretend that he was a child. He brought up our love story again and again. "Do you remember?" I said I did.

But memory is not the currency of affection. I listened to him talk about our past like someone was reading me a story about another girl. A girl who had no home, a girl who didn't know where she belonged, a girl with clean hands and nice hair who ate at fancy restaurants and raced through canyon roads in expensive cars. He never mentioned a girl in cutoffs and heavy work boots with tan arms and dirt on her knees. He didn't see me at the farm in his memories. That wasn't part of the character I played for him or part of the character he imagined for me. I wouldn't have to play anything anymore. I wouldn't have a role. My stomach rolled as it had on the bridge before I jumped with Cyrus and then I let myself go, cutting away everything that had held me to our love story.

By morning, Jayden's face glowed white with fear. I made him breakfast. He pushed it around his plate and went out to the porch to smoke. I watched that he did not go flying off it. Instead he just stood there, looking straight out into the distance. I called to him and he turned, trudging back into the house with his curls tumbling over his eyes. In the dark back room he packed up his clothing and his favorite books into two big suitcases. He told me to throw away everything else: the air mattress, the cinderblocks that supported his desk, the posters on the walls. After leaving his suitcases by the door he sat with his legs crossed, watching through the window with the cat as his parents hiked up the stairs to the apartment.

I don't remember the rest of the day. I think we all went for a walk. Some of the trees were starting to bud. I probably paced with my hands behind my back, watching the cracks under my feet. I think his mom took me aside and hugged me and whispered into my neck how grateful she was. I remember hearing car doors slam. Jayden's dad drove his car back down the coast.

Jayden folded himself into his mom's rental. We waved at each other. I looked down from the porch as they pulled out of the parking lot, over the hill, and out of sight.

I thought of all the possible endings I had imagined for us—a quiet death in our marriage bed, or a poetic separation like the couple in Bob Dylan's "Tangled Up in Blue," saying goodbye on the edge of the highway in the pouring rain. But not this quiet split. I watched the road for a while until I was sure they weren't coming back then I slid the glass door shut behind me, and stood in the emptiness of the apartment.

Quickly, as if to rid myself of him completely, I bundled Jayden's cast-off clothing into black trash bags and brought them to a consignment store in the city. My body felt charged with the need to start fresh. I hauled the heavy bags in from the street and slung them up on the counter. A teenage clerk tossed most of it into donation bins, Jayden's stained T-shirts, his ripped sweatpants, but kept enough to hand me twenty dollars. I spent it all on a half-dozen huge, cream-filled cupcakes at the upscale bakery down the block. They were set like gemstones in a pink cardboard box and carrying them back to my car I felt changed, as if I cast just one shadow now, instead of the two that had followed me all season.

Back in the apartment, I opened the lid on the cupcake box gingerly lest I scrape their beautiful swirled frosting, topped with sugar-dusted rose petals. I ate one, then another, until I didn't feel like celebrating anymore, my heart racing with sugar. I drowned in the bed, small and alone and very tired, my ears ringing with silence. Guilt came like the cat and sat on my chest as I slept. I dreamed of looking down into the heart of the earth.

Taking a seed inventory is the last job of the year. I pack all the seeds that the farm owns into the back of my car so I can count them in the warmth of my apartment. Sitting on my carpet in the pink glow of my living room paint, with the cat weaving around me, I open one plastic box at a time. Seed smells fill the apartment, the scent of cilantro, pumpkin, bitter tomato calling themselves back to life.

The seed packets are sloppy and askew in their cases, thrown back in during busy spring and summer afternoons when a cold beer or the river was calling and there were better things to do than organize seeds. My fingerprints stain some of the paper, marked dirty swirls on the white labels. Other hands are there too, Nick and Luke's on the bags of the crops that were placed directly into the field by our tractor-drawn seeder. Their smudges cover the spinach, carrot, and beet packets while mine

are all over the smaller seeds, like the tomato and broccoli that I had carefully planted in flats in the heat of the
greenhouse.

Before examining their contents, I organize each box
by plant and variety. I toss out empty bags and fold the
tops over others that had been left open. Then I set about
counting them. I start with the tomatoes. On my laptop,
I create a spreadsheet to record the plant, variety, number
of seeds, and age of the seed. Some seeds go bad quickly
over the course of a season while others last for years.
If something is too old the germination rate will be low
and those flats will waste space in the greenhouse. Those
older seeds are donated or tossed in the compost.

Carefully, I open each packet and look inside. The
loose seeds roll to the edge or into the corners of the
paper packets so sometimes I pour them into my palm
and count them one by one. Other times I'd simply weigh
the packets on a postal scale. The seed company prints
how many seeds make up an ounce so I can weigh and
then multiply to reach a final count. After a few hours, my
hands become expert at this task and can guess a weight
nearly as accurately as the scale can calculate it. Some are
light as feathers. Others require a strong arm to lift.

The tomato varieties bring me back to August, to
their rainbow of sliced flesh on the tasting table. Red,
green, purple, pink, striped beauties shaped like hearts
or strange flowers. Their seeds are small and tear-shaped.
Some varieties are fuzzy and others have flat, polished
seeds. I fold their packets up tenderly. I know I will be the
person to open them in the spring and pour them back

out into my palm at the seeding table in the greenhouse. I will be there, seeding these tomatoes, and they'll bloom and break in the dark cheek of the compost, each cell containing a tiny, arching plant.

The light draws thin and fades as I count. I begin at sunrise and end at the final rays of weak, early winter light, getting up off the carpet to stretch and brew tea. The cat sits in one box and then another until she grows tired of my work, and, having tried out all the boxes, retreats to the bedroom. I sort the spreadsheet alphabetically, artichoke to zucchini. This final tally takes me nearly two days. By the time I am finished the bags are as neatly stacked in their compartments as they were the first day that Luke opened them in late winter to seed the early tomatoes. I send the document to him so that he can order seeds for the next season using my numbers as inventory.

Another thing happens while I count the seeds. I plant myself in the future. By the end of that week, I have touched every seed that will go into the ground or into a flat of soil mix next year and for years into the future, every small flake and sphere that will someday be a ripe pea, or heavy red pepper, or a bunch of sweet basil. Every seed is a promise. And I am part of that pact.

The seeds say, *Keep going. Right now, we are nothing. We are small but soon we will break and grow lush and tall.* They promise me that things will change. When I go to bed that night with the plastic boxes near my mattress, I am sleeping with the future of forty acres packed into neat white packets, dreaming of being what they are meant to become.

GROWTH

Below ground, roots are healing and threading out into the soil. Rain pulses like blood through the plant's veins. All the long hours of the day, the sun will guide it towards maturity as if, all along, there was only one perfect future.

CHAPTER SEVENTEEN

Before entering the pawnshop, I stood under its ragged awning as cold rain washed over Portland's hills. One last time, I slipped the ring onto my finger. I resented its tight fit and the way the metal warmed quickly on my hand. That ring was a physical form of a promise that had been broken a hundred ways but with it on my finger, I couldn't help but feel a flush of hope. *No.* I'd prepared for this hesitation. There was no turning back.

I swung my purse over my shoulder and pulled my jacket tails down straight. I performed all these little acts of strength, these acts of willful editing that I had learned to mask my growing sense of hopelessness, an emptiness so vast that I woke some mornings before class wondering why I couldn't just sleep all day. But I'd haul myself up out of the sheets and shower and dress and be the first girl in lecture, sitting straight in the front of the room with my reading marked up and a big smile for the professor. That girl took a lot of work to maintain. I'd get tired and have to readjust my smile. Sometimes I'd slip back to the apartment for a nap so that in my evening classes I could, again, perform my act.

Even out on the edge of town, pocked with pawn-shops and strip clubs, I wouldn't let it up. I didn't want to slip in public and break apart. I caught a glimpse of myself in the reflection of the glass door; my face was wet with rain, and my eyes were huge and dark, almost animal. I looked like a girl on the brink of jumping, or a woman taking flight into the night where she might transform into a wolf, or an owl, or any other honest, beautiful thing.

The door jingled behind me and I became that girl I was dreaming of, boldly shifting into the skin of the successful college student, the top of her class, the oldest in her family, the girl who wore real pearls and J.Crew and kept her books in a vintage leather bag and never, ever, fucked up. It wasn't hard to be that girl for the few seconds it took me to walk down the worn carpet to the cash register.

I was the only person in the shop, with its bleak over-head lighting and walls hung with rifles and Xboxes, and I hoped the man behind the register would acknowledge my bravery in some small way for walking in like I had; maybe he'd straighten up as I had stood tall before open-ing the door. But he only kept his eyes fixed on my gold as I screwed the ring off my finger and set it, with a cold cling, on the glass counter.

My hand quickly forgot the weight of the gold. Lying out on the counter, the ring looked like an empty zero.

The man pointed above him to a whiteboard where he'd scrawled the day's prices for precious metals and I nodded approvingly at his offer as he weighed the gold on a digital scale. He slipped the ring into a plastic bag that looked like it could contain evidence from a crime scene and then my ring disappeared into a safe with other rings and watches and broken promises. The man counted out two crisp hundred-dollar bills into my palm, which I folded and slipped into my purse. It was exactly enough money to get me home. I signed my name on a line and, pulling my collar up around my neck, walked back out into the cool rain.

In the car, driving back to my apartment, I listened to "Take Me Home, Country Roads" by John Denver. As rain blurred my vision through the windshield and tears streaked my mascara, I sang along with the CD like I used to sing along with my Dad when he'd play the song on his guitar before my sister and I went to sleep as little girls. When the song ended, I pushed repeat. Most days I felt a sort of itchy bleakness, as if tomorrow and the next day would be forever exactly the same. It was the sort of feeling that made me look out windows for a long time, or stare into the faces of my friends whose framed pictures cluttered my mantel. It wasn't the sort of thing I could rid myself of easily, this restlessness. Crying felt almost productive; like the medieval surgeon with his lancet bleeding a patient of ill humor, I thought maybe my tears would draw out my sorrow. There was no one to watch me fall apart. I rubbed my empty ring finger nervously as I drove, thinking the same thing I did every night as

I moved through the city: that all the people, in all the bright warm homes were happier than me.

I came home to the one dark window in a tall wall of lights. My boots echoed up the stairwell, clumping one step at a time until I reached the top floor where, at the turn of the hallway, my black cat sat by the side of the doorframe's window watching the stairwell with the ferocity of a guard dog. Sometimes, at night, I would hear her growling at that window and would sneak, on tiptoes, across the carpeted hall to double-check the locks and the deadbolt and watch shadowy legs slipping down the stairs.

The cat knew me by sight. She welcomed me home by rubbing her face on my wet boots and weaving between my legs.

Jayden had been gone for a week now. He'd once worn a ring that matched mine. I didn't, I realized, even know where his ring was. Did he leave it in California at his father's beach house? Did he toss it out in the trash after our fight in Boston's Logan Airport? Maybe he pawned it for drug money or threw it off the top of the canyon where we used to drive at night to feel the Santa Ana winds hot on our faces. I thought that he might still have it, hidden somewhere, and that he might slip it on when he was high or joyfully drunk on gin and remember the evening we gave each other zeros cast from gold. It was the first time he ever saw fireflies. Even that memory seemed so long ago. I imagined us smaller, as if we were still children. I was eighteen and he was seventeen and we lay on my childhood bed watching the fireflies

rise up from the fields and said words we didn't understand like *forever*.

Now, four years later, I felt guilty for pawning that
last bit of our love. He was probably too high to care
if I told him anyways, I thought. He said the pain still
wouldn't go away. I'd gotten used to the strange division
that separated my space from his and even with him gone
I hadn't touched anything into the back room. I was a
little embarrassed to remember the first day we moved
in, how long we spent picking out the pea green paint for
the living room and the electric salmon for the kitchen,
and how we'd tenderly unpacked our books and paintings. That first night we smoked a joint up the chimney
and ate Chinese takeout while sitting cross-legged on the
floor. Now I felt always like I was tripping over our ghosts.

What I hated about the place was how lonely I felt.
Coming from school or from the lights on the freeway,
the apartment shrunk the world down and became cell-
like. The walls of the cell shut down quickly and I felt
the bravery I'd built up before walking into the pawnshop
melt away. My shoulders slumped. I wiped my face and
drew away streaks of makeup. I'd started to drink wine
to get me there faster. That Frost poem, "Stopping by
Woods on a Snowy Evening," was read a hundred times
to me growing up in New England. But I thought it was
more about searching for an end than a nice old man and
his horses walking through a storm, bells chiming.

In the bright salmon-colored kitchen, I scraped
together scrambled eggs and an English muffin and
poured my coffee cup full of deep red wine. Rain dripped

down the inside of the chimney, turning the cinderblocks a darker grey. It was nights like this that the loneliness of a city startled me. In the house where I grew up, I could hear coyotes and neighborhood dogs barking and howling, or the brook running full with melt water, or the snowplow scraping the frozen dirt of our road in the deep of the night. In Oregon, I could hear people all around me, but I'd never felt so alone.

I poured myself another coffee mug of red wine and sat with the cat on the edge of the king-sized bed that dominated the living room floor. Once it was our bed, now it was just mine. Tomorrow I'd deposit the cash in my bank account and use it to get home. It could buy gas or an airline ticket. What mattered was that I'd be home. I'd be where I was wanted. In the light of my laptop screen, I could see my own blue face in the glass porch doors. Out past my reflection, above the glare of the streetlights, the golden statue of an angel atop the Mormon temple pointed his trumpet triumphantly back east. I knew the angel was beckoning towards Joseph Smith's birthplace a few towns to the west of where I grew up but I thought, maybe, he was showing me the way home.

To the east over the Cascades, two thousand miles across the country, the farm sat on the banks of the Connecticut River whose water ran brown and slow in its old banks under the ice. The fields came right up to the river's edge and spread flat and silty up towards the old red barn where time and centuries of snow-weight had buckled the roofline against the soft folds of the Green Mountains. I closed my eyes and flew there in my mind,

like a plane on the jet stream, or a migrating bird. I knew
the land around the farm and the fields so well I could
walk it in dead darkness, I could walk it blindfolded. I
had measured that land with my feet, my hands and the
stretch of my legs. In that soil, I thought dreamily, there
were particles of stardust and glacier-ground granite as
well as my own blood, sweat, and tears.

I had never been to the farm in February, so I imagined
it. I lived in those daydreams. They were the rations of
my days. I knew that storms wrapped the fields in thick
blankets of snow. The greenhouses became rounded hills
until Luke or Nick took out a long rake and skimmed the
powder off. Snow built buttresses up to the greenhouses'
sides so that early in the spring six feet of it might still
climb the plastic, making the spaces like tunnels.

I knew that in February the first seeds were started.
Just a few flats of tomatoes, not enough to warrant firing
up the propane in the big greenhouse. In a few weeks, as
the seeding list expanded and March grew closer, Luke
would lay beside the furnaces and reach the long tip of
a grill lighter into the belly of those machines, searching
blindly for the pilot light. They ignited with a click and
a burst of propane and the furnaces would rattle to life
for the first time. The metal grew warm to the touch
before the fans turned on and heat worked its way slowly
through the greenhouses.

Sometimes, during cold years, Luke or Nick would lay
in a sleeping bag on the cement floor and light a torpedo
heater every few hours for extra warmth. In that deep
chill, the banks of snow on the plastic skin insulated the

space. On bitter nights in Oregon, even I slept anxiously. I dreamt of the tender first leaves of plants shriveling black from frost. Sometimes I woke with a start and went to my window and looked out over Portland, goosebumps prickling my skin. I knew that the first seeds needed to be protected and tended carefully. They were loved better than all the rest, like only children. Those early plants spoke of unbroken promises for a perfect season.

There were moments when I forgot the past. I forgot what came before and thought only of where I was going. It was soothing, really, to float untethered through an afternoon. But other days I got trapped in my memories, circling back to the same film reel of moments over and over until I couldn't help but miss Jayden or the landscape of our time together. I collected them and tried to lock them away as old mementos but sometimes I couldn't help myself from looking back through them.

I would think of the view of Mount Hood in the sunrise from the apartment in Portland, and how it had shocked us so on our first morning in the city, or the smell of Jayden's father's beach house where the waves came up under his bedroom and filled the home with the scent of dark rocks and salt. I'd fall into daydreams of our happiest times and jolt myself out because I sensed myself fading from the vitality of the moment, loosing my drive forward. I'd recall his pills, his rages, his betrayal, as if it was an antidote.

I hadn't heard from Jayden since he'd written to me on Facebook to say that he was attending outpatient therapy at a recovery center. He'd been creating poems too. He mentioned strange, beautiful poems that I understood later as the reflections of a healing but still toxic mind. He was between worlds, although he said only that he spent his afternoons in art therapy and his evenings on the beach or walking the canyon roads.

Returning to my apartment one day from class I found a package from Jayden sitting on the front step. It was a slim brown paper mailer and I opened it cautiously. Inside was a small chapbook of poetry which he'd written and self-published. The poems themselves were tiny, little seashells of stanzas stacked carefully on each other. He'd inscribed the copy to me with a note that said *For Megan, As Always.* Folded in an envelope was a printed letter. The letter was quickly drafted and honest, devoid of the high language that I felt, secretly, confused his poems. He'd written these poems in recovery. He hoped I remembered him well. I folded the note and slipped it back into the chapbook and, without reading his poems, placed it on the shelf, between the volumes. I wanted them to rest there, hidden. I wanted them to remain unread.

During the week the map of my days felt close and efficient. Home to school and back home again. I kept my routine close, crossing the same paths daily with the kind of ritual I'd learned at the farm to help keep a wild mind steady. Ritual, I knew, brightened the darkness. I hardly noticed spring come to the hills that season. In Oregon, it seemed to me that every tree bloomed some pastel shade of cloud. I had once loved to look from my balcony at the watercolored hills of Portland—pink, yellow, white, soft purple, all charged with the electric green of new leaves. But that spring I was already gone. If I wasn't in class I was in the library or reading at my desk. If I was done with homework, I was asleep or drinking wine to tighten the walls of the world. I wanted to be confined, boxed in. It felt easier to live, as I had with Jayden, in a fixed universe. In it, I knew all the rules, all the variables. I didn't feel suffocated. I felt safe.

On the weekends, when I had less to occupy my days, I was drawn to the city. Portland was the perfect setting for my particular breed of loneliness and depression. Its stony downtown, its graffitied iron bridges, its rusted wings soaring with neon, its fallen brick along the waterfront all felt costume made, an urban reflection of the grey-toned flatness that colored my vision. I'd walked the city streets near Christmas and felt the place golden. I'd driven it closed down in winter snow, binary in the blanket of white, and it had seemed quaint, like a large Victorian village. But without Jayden, the city seemed to be a sad stranger. I walked it and it watched me, silently, neither welcoming me in nor shutting me out.

Maybe it knew, or the passing people on the streets did, that Portland wasn't where I belonged. Maybe the city itself could sense my homesickness, my pull back east to Cedar Circle. *What was I even doing here?* I wondered, wandering the warrens of Powell's Books, hoping, as I always did, for a slim volume to offer some redemption, a map out. Jayden and I had chosen to apply to the college in the city because we both loved the writings of a deceased poet who had once led their English department. We'd felt that his energy might still reside at the school, might somehow have seeped into the spruce and estate rooms of that campus. Every morning the poet had woken and gone for a mile run through the college roads, lined with looming evergreens. Perhaps his ghost still wove a path there, sprouting words like flower bulbs. We'd been so hungry to create that we'd forgotten to live.

The poet was dead and buried and the campus was ordinary. I had been, since our first semester, a history major, having been repulsed from the English department by a bitter American Literature class which felt like a botched full-body dissection rather than a celebration of the words I loved. If I wrote anything at all it was research papers. I did draw though, self-portrait after self-portrait, inked out in the dim light of high windows, sketched in the gloom of winter in the Pacific Northwest. But these reflections hardly felt like art. Seeing my own face sickened me. It was a struggle to sit through life drawing, repeating the same ragged lines of my features in new mediums.

To make it through the studio sessions I'd pretend that I wasn't the girl looking back from the mirror. Instead, I'd imagine that the glass was a window and the face was that of a model. A girl gazing blankly that had a name I didn't know. She looked a little bit like me but wasn't me after all. She was too sad-looking, too pale. Nothing like the girl I imagined myself to be—tan, strong, and dirty. That girl looked back at the world through confident eyes, not the sad, full moons I drew with charcoals and watercolor's leached pigment.

There wasn't much for me to do on campus during the weekends, and I preferred taking my art supplies home over working in the empty studio. Besides the bookstore and the streets of downtown where I might sit inside a café and drink a steaming cup of tea, my only regular outing to the city was the Saturday farmers market. The crowded space along the river walk filled with food stalls, craftsmen and farmers. As cherry blossoms drifted like pink snow, I wandered alone through the crowd, stopping in front of tables stocked with spring vegetables. At Cedar Circle, it was my job to stand behind the table at the farmers market and sell our products to Saturday crowds. But here I wasn't the farmer. Spring came early in the Willamette Valley and the market was flush with bright radishes, vibrant bunches of greens, and the first greenhouse tomatoes. I'd brush my fingers along the vegetables, remembering the texture of each plant and how, if I was working behind the counter under the shade of pop-up tent, I'd toss my voice out into a line of customers, reeling them in for more.

Before heading back to my apartment I'd task myself with finding the best tomatoes at the farmers market. It was a challenge to see if my farm girl skills were still sharp. The task also allowed me a reason to visit every farm booth and table, and put my hands in contact with vegetable skin and fruit flesh. I can't imagine how I must have looked to the vendors. A girl going table to table, fondling their tomatoes, weighing each fruit in her palms, lifting one to her nose, inspecting another in the light outside the tent, searching out rare gems in the heaps of riches with an expression on her face somewhere between sorrow and revelation.

This ritual was my only connection to the fruits of the earth. My hands were book hands, keyboard hands, wrists and back sore from stooping, eyes aching for squinting at the small print of history textbooks and the glowing blue screens of laptops. My hands were dirty sometimes with charcoal, or ink, or my own thin sweat in the gym, but only on Saturdays were my hands those of a farm girl.

It took an expert touch to feel the difference between ripeness and bruise. It required an understanding of the deep time of plants. Which was ready today and which would be ready in three days? I'd fill bags with tomatoes of all sizes and colors, some as small as quail eggs, others larger than softballs. They were black, gold, striped, neon green, deep purple, and ivory. Back in the lonely walls of my apartment, where Jayden's things still smelled slightly of his sweat in the back room and the farm haunted me from framed photos, I'd lay my treasures in a wooden bowl on the breakfast bar, arranging them like a florist so that each color sparked. The cat would sniff them, savoring the smell of wild things in our urban home. She'd flick her tail at me as I reached into the bowl and drew up one orb, its skin tight and glossy, brushed with sugar and pollen dust. I'd eat them sliced and sprinkled with flakes of sea salt or lay them on toast drizzled in olive oil. When I was very hungry and couldn't stop myself, I'd eat them like apples, whole, from side to side, letting the jeweled seeds drip down my wrists.

Later in the evening, drunk on wine and sticky with tomato juice, I talked to Luke through a photo of him sitting on the tailgate of his truck, surrounded by artichokes. The picture rested on the mantel and I'd lean against the woodwork as if I was resting on a table in the barn, chatting with him after work, a glass of wine heavy in my hand. In the image, Luke holds two of the largest artichokes up to my camera, smiling for the pure joy of having grown artichokes in Vermont. I could imagine the smell of the day: wood shaving and carpentry tools from his truck, the bitter blood of those thistle plants, a watermelon sliced open on the processing table, flooding sugar. I could feel its heat and shimmer.

I told Luke that I remembered that day. I remembered taking that picture. We picked the artichokes together, cutting each with a serrated knife and slipping it into the fabric bags slung over our shoulders. By the end of the row, the bag pulled me heavily to one side and I had to lean the other way, against it, to stay upright. The tall plants prickled with thorns and our legs scratched pink from brushing against them. Each cut stem produced a clear, acidic sap that thickened to black on our hands and seeped into our skin so that all day we smelled of the thistle-bite of artichokes. Sweat rolled down my face, down my lower back. The sun sat on my shoulder, burning.

"Look at this one," we would say when we found a big one. We would smile at our success, and at the wonder of it all. An annual artichoke, grown ripe and full in the brief summer of Vermont representing the power of the compost we had mixed into each hole, how the soil had become thick and dark, full of microscopic life. "That was a good day," I said to his picture.

"Luke," I added, toasting his picture with my mug of wine, "I need to come back to the farm." His smile remained fixed, the artichokes in his hands raised like talismans. The wine made my body soft but my mind was set. I felt myself moving forward, rushing toward the fields. I just needed to survive a few more months. I was so close to flight I could hear feathers shifting. At night I fell asleep to the sensation of rising.

⁂

In the early morning, Luke watches his girlfriend drive away to work. Sunlight comes in bright and clear from the south-facing windows on the front of The Yellow House. The pine floorboards and ceiling turn to honey. The whole kitchen melts in the slight warmth of the sun. Luke stands in it for a while. He can feel the power growing in it each day. The sun draws closer, like a warm hand on his cheek. Coffee steams from his mug and the steam rises in the light of the kitchen, creating patterns there in its swirling tendrils that remind him of the fog coming off the river in June or hovering above the rows in October when the ground is warmer than the air.

First Luke opens the plastic boxes by his desk. They hold all the seeds he has planned out and ordered during the winter. He can smell them through the crisp white paper bags, each seed a small promise. The flecks of fennel sweet as licorice, the fat pumpkin seeds slightly oily with the sweetness of squash flesh. All the smells mix together in the plastic boxes so when he opens the lid he thinks of driving through the fields at high summer, passing one crop, then another.

He's organized the seed packets so that each vegetable has a cardboard slip in front of it, upon which he's written their names. Behind the "Tomato" tag stand bags of Geronimo, Celebrity, Sungold, Valley Girl, Brandywine, Yellow Pear, and dozens more. Their names call up the fruit: the pink weight of Brandywine, sweet as a Merlot; the candy pop of a Sungold cherry in the mouth. There are field tomatoes, grown for their abundance; and heirlooms, for their novelty; cherry tomatoes, for kids to pick.

Next, he opens the white paper packets and rattles the seeds in his palm. He pours them into a bag made of window screens and boils them for a few minutes over his stove. Hot water burns away trace bacteria that might have come with the seeds. He lays them out to dry on a paper towel, golden and slightly fuzzy. Two days ago, he carried in bags of compost and let them thaw in the mudroom. This morning they are room temperature and soft. He unfolds his knife and cuts into the top of the bag. The smell of soil, the first of the season, comes up on the blade. It is black and moist, a complex stew of mulch, minerals, composted plants and animals. Under the pool of sun in front of the windows, he sets out a plastic folding table and fills six black flats with compost. Each cell is shaped like a honeycomb.

Sunlight warms the soil on the table by the window. He pours the dried tomato seeds into a tap seeder and taps out one seed over each cell. If two fall, he pulls up one with a set of tweezers. Each tap forms a prayer. He doesn't speak but he imagines words. One at a time, he thinks *bounty, red, health, warmth, success, market, juice, flower, bees, summer, sweat.*

He can feel the weight of a full tray of tomatoes in his arms. He can almost touch their tight skins, dusted with tomato pollen. He can see them displayed in the farm stand and the market in town, so red they almost glow. He can smell the close air in the greenhouse at night when he will go out to check on the plants after a few beers while dusk settles between the aisles and heat rises from the ground.

When the flats are filled, he lightly sifts more compost over the top to cover the seeds. They need to fight a little for the light. With a mister, he sprays them wet. The water clings to the glass window and breaks light into tiny rainbows. His kitchen smells of soil and water. Those two elements meet for the first time this year and create a chemical equation read in the nose as life. Luke looks at his palms, sees them blackened with compost, and feels the return of the growing season. He knows himself again as a farmer and not just a cultivator of dreams.

Once a day he rotates the flats so they will germinate evenly. At night he covers them with clear plastic domes. The soil breathes warmth and the domes perspire so in the morning he removes the coverings and waters them again with the mister. He tends to them three or four times a day: water, rotate, water, cover. They bind him to the farm again.

Then suddenly, one morning, the surface of the soil rises in one cell. By noon the arched back of a sprout pushes through and then the whole flat breaks open and green starts lift their first leaves to the sun. Their rising looks like whales breaching; joy bursts in their expansion, in their reaching for the light. They stretch toward the window. Little hairs develop on their stems and they begin to smell of tomatoes.

Outside, snow slips down the greenhouses. The road darkens slick with ice and the sky falls so cold it takes your breath away. But the first tomato plants follow only the sun, tracking its short path through the southern sky. Every dawn it rises stronger and climbs higher, and the seedlings grow with it until they are thickened and ready for larger pots.

In February the season starts indoors, in the kitchen, so personal that Luke will refer to these plants all year as *his tomatoes*. They begin the rituals again: soil and water, seed and light, and dirty hands.

CHAPTER EIGHTEEN

Go back, go back, became a mantra as regular as my heart-beat. In the grocery store, I touched the produce, stirring scent as I pinched off a leaf of cilantro and crushed it between my thumb and palm, lifting tomatoes to my nose to smell their ripeness, covering my fingers with the sap of green onion tops.

All this, I thought. *I can grow all this*. From seed to bunching I could imagine the flats in the greenhouse, the cold water of the washing sink. I knew each vegetable's beauty in the field at sunrise, fresh as spring stars. I knew the sound that rain made as it fell on their leaves: green onion's hollow drops, the gentle collapse of cilantro, the *drip, drip, drip* off ripe tomatoes. But there in Portland, ghosts and dark things walked through my days. Jayden's room remained closed off; it smelled of his unwashed hair and I didn't like how present it made him feel.

One night, walking back from the gym across the road from my apartment, I saw him drifting through the parking lot. His hands rested in his pajama pants pockets.

He wore his favorite soccer team's jersey and his hair tumbled in clean light curls around his face. He looked my way sadly, and then shifted his gaze back down to the pavement, his shoulders sloping as if his head was suddenly too heavy. I knew that stance perfectly—his lazy, bad posture.

I stopped and stared. The lights from the parking lot created bright islands between the darkness. Above me, the stars and moon dimmed in the glare of the city. Sweat dried on my skin in the cold night air. I formed his name with my tongue but didn't speak it. The sound might have made him stop and turn to me. Instead, Jayden walked away, into a place between lights. I watched a while waiting for him to return. I have never seen a ghost so clearly and I still can't say if he was a phantom or if he visited, one last time, to say goodbye.

What was he doing here? I wondered. *What does he want?*

His eyes were full of regret, big moons of forgiveness. He slouched like the schoolboy I had loved in Michigan, all words and book pages and inky hands. I checked the locks. I pulled down all the shades, even the one to the porch just in case his ghost flew up the three stories and rested in the patio chairs, smoking American Spirits and gazing down at the city lights.

⚘

The farm roads ripple with ruts and puddles. Sawdust, electrical wires, and other junk from winter construction projects collect around the edges of the barn. Boards lay over the lawn so that we can walk from door to door without sinking or slipping in the mud. Nick has hung a galvanized steel sap bucket on the maple in the front yard and the sap drops, *ping, ping, ping*, into it, as the tree's heartbeat rises toward the warm sun. Snow still pools in shaded spots but the sun has exposed most of the fields and they radiate heat, brown and golden. Little rivers run through them. The whole central road has become a series of lakes and running water, shining under the sun. The soil's ice melts and casts off its winter clothes, revealing blank pages of potential, the start of a new season of growth. With the snow gone I can see the shape of each field and the turns in the road. Those acres no longer belong to some frozen wildness, a thing without structure. They are a farm once again.

Luke and Nick clean out the shed and move the big plow truck, billowing diesel smoke, from its winter home under cover to its summer place among the tractors by the tool shop. I hug them. The winter can seem so long that a body forgets the shape of a friend. I embraced their dirty wool coats and stained canvas, the sawdust, oil, dirt, sun smell in the collars of their jackets, their sweat blooming on the brim of their baseball caps.

We walk through the greenhouses, where Rosemary and Judy are standing at the worktable, placing tiny geraniums in larger pots of soil. Their faces flush with sweat and their noses are just a little pink, burnt bright across the nose. Classical music plays low from their old radio with crinkled aluminum foil antenna, bathing the first flower blooms with sonatas and symphonies.

Inside the greenhouses, it is over 80 degrees. Two big fans draw in cool air from outside and pull it through the body of space, over the heads of small begonias, daisies, and verbenas, and out the raised garage door in the back. The air inside smells wet and soil-rich, sweetened with geranium's bitter poison and sticky petunia oils. Itchi sprawls out on the wooden worktable, sunbathing. I rub his grey belly. In response he opens and closes each big paw, the dark crescent of his claws reaching out then retracting. Deep in his belly is a low rumble of a purr, like distant thunder.

Across the road in the greenhouse by the tractor shed, Luke has hung a plastic partition in the back so that only that small space can be heated. The first vegetable starts sprout in this protected area. He and Nick lead me there, spilling words over each other about all the changes in the year to come, how we will do things better, bigger this time, with new varieties, new staff, and field plans.

Luke holds up the plastic sheet for us so we can slip inside. In the back of the greenhouse, heat shimmers hot and bright. It smells slightly like the bleach they have used to clean the floors and the plastic skin; a good clean start. Flats of onions rest on the south side tables, each labeled as Copra, Gold Coin, or Red Wing. Specks of mica and vermiculite in the potting mix shimmer in the heat. In the back, by the furnace, a box wrapped in black plastic rests on a cart with the lid propped slightly open. A temperature probe dangles out the side. Luke lifts the lid off and I peek in.

The first tomatoes, which he seeded carefully in his kitchen, have grown into five-inch plants. He picks one up to show me, carefully separating it from the embrace of neighboring leaves. He grafted them a few days ago, meshing two varieties together to make one hardy plant. He hands the constructed start to me so I can examine the scar where the two plants met. With a razor blade, he cut a diagonal slash through the stem of each seeding, threw away the soil ball of the fruit stock and the leaves of the other. Then, surgically, he laid the two scars together, perfectly lining up the green veins of the bottom plant to the green veins of the top. A small clip locks them together. Through the clear plastic, I can see the incision. The leaves on the grafted plant are thick and healthy, a sign that the graft has worked and the plant is drawing nutrients up from the roots and down from the leaves through reconnected tissue. I gently pass it back to Luke. He places it in the black box with the others where it will continue to grow, improved despite its scar, eagerly rising towards the light.

CHAPTER NINETEEN

My French Revolution history class sat silently. No one wanted to discuss the reading from the past week; piles of it, dense and tedious, punctuated by moments of horrendous violence. It wasn't the kind of thing anyone would want to chat about first thing in the morning. The day was dawning dark outside the high basement windows. The professor took off his glasses and rubbed the corners of his eyes, bearing out silence like a weight on his shoulders. The air around the table grew heavy. He told us, as if we were suddenly his friends, that his teaching contract hadn't been renewed for the next semester and that he would be moving on. At home, his wife avoided him. She didn't want to pack up again. His face looked raw, like he had been wiping away tears all night with rough paper towels.

"It's a hard life," he said, and I worried he might start to cry. He hoped none of us wanted to become academics. "There's nothing for you," he said. "What do you all want to do when you graduate?" Hoping, I thought, to spark any kind of conversation. One of the boys shrugged, he hadn't thought about it. One girl wanted to teach; the professor dipped his head in sorrow. Most of the students didn't know yet. They'd go to graduate school and figure it out.

The professor sunk lower into his chair. "So much money," he said, "for nothing."

I sat to his left side and spoke last in the circle. My books stood before me in a neat stack. I had arranged them nervously during his confession while the room thickened with tension and I hoped that they'd act as some kind of fortress, repelling his gaze. But now he was peering over the top of my ramparts with sad, bloodshot eyes.

"I'm going to drop out of school and become a farmer," I said. I hadn't spoken those words out loud before although I'd formed them so many times in my head that they seemed like a constant scream. The phase fell out of my lips without thinking and I watched how my response altered the faces of my classmates. Their blank stares jumped up to meet me, suddenly excited. My professor's eyes grew wide and he sat up straight. I felt the statement growing outside of me, on the table, like a plant rooted before me, twisting out with the vigor of a pumpkin vine, eager for expansion.

The professor adjusted the glasses on the bridge of his nose, looking, I thought, like he'd gotten ahold of himself. He nodded at me, a short clipped nod of approval. "That's the bravest thing I've heard," he said. "I wish you all the luck in the world."

Those words sprouted in my heart.

I'm going to drop out of school and become a farmer. I said it again to myself in the uncomfortable silence of the classroom and it became real. The dream took a shape: a squash, from seed to blossom to fruit. It grew so tangible I could almost hold it in my hand.

***

What was frozen becomes liquid. Ice and snow and frost change forms during the day, like fairytale characters, and then back again in the night, buckling the roads, quaking the fields until finally they are water spirits, flood spirits, cutting courses through yards and driveways, through pastures and foundations, following the simple pull of gravity down to the lowest point. The Connecticut takes it all into its wide banks—stream, brook, river, trickles, spring—and rises as it races down through the states to the ocean. It is a season of mess and mud, false starts and surprises. One week I am sunburnt badly pruning blueberries in 80-degree weather and the next a greenhouse of seedlings freezes to death when a blizzard knocks open the north door and roars through the space all night, blowing out the furnaces' pilot lights like birthday candles. It is a month of change and movement.

Even when the fields finally open, we have to wait until the last hard frost—sometime around the end of the month—before we plant, because some crops are too tender for cold nights and bitter winds. Basil turns brown when the weather drops below 45 degrees; tomatoes, peppers, and eggplants simply won't grow if the soil is less than 65 degrees; melon vines will shrivel, sweet potato slips blacken, cucumbers and squash plants fall limp over the ground. It's a waiting game. The transplants grow eagerly under the protection of the greenhouse plastic. We weigh weather and experience against risk and the roots push and fill out against the small cells, sucking up nutrients until they simply must go out.

The wire tables in Greenhouse 4, by the tractor shops, are nearly full so I begin each Monday by moving flats and trays of plants around to make space for that week's seeding. In a miniature way, I am organizing the fields of the future, placing crops together as they will lay in their rows. Planting time starts as a series of transitions: from pot to soil, hand watering to rain, fan to wind, plastic to the sky. *Welcome to the real world,* I say, as I carry out starts to the flatbeds where they will remain for a few days under the sky, wind, and sun, still pot-bound but hand-watered. When they are hardened off the leaves change slightly—they thicken, they wilt less and stand straighter. Times of transition—greenhouse to field, season to season—are always the most vulnerable and tender. I speak to the flats of plants as I water them gently on the trailers, back and forth, telling them they are tough and ready for their new lives. They say nothing in return but soak up the cool water from the hose and rustle in the spring breeze.

Once I clear enough space inside, I have waves of squash, cucumbers, basil, and lettuce to seed. These waves are called successive plantings, planned so that as one row of lettuce is harvested another is ready right behind it. This means a steady schedule of seeding. Luke creates a chart in the off-season on an Excel spreadsheet, which he prints and binds in a plastic folder. Every week begins with a new list of crops to seed and each Monday it is my job to open the three-ring binder and start at the top of the list. I walk back across the road to grab the folder from the office in the barn and then search through the seedboxes until I find the right packets. They smell faintly like their future selves. I return to the warmth of the greenhouse and spread the white paper seed packets on the worktable. First, I open the folder and begin writing tags with a marker. One tag per flat, repeated a hundred times until words like 'corn' or 'onion' become a meaningless collection of symbols. I write until I can only imagine the plant as an object, as something with weight and smell, nameless and essential.

A radio hangs from a piece of twine and the smooth voices of NPR murmur in and out of focus. The news of the outside world drifts by. I take off my shirt and work in my bikini, pulling my baseball cap down to shade my eyes. I mix compost with water in an old porcelain bathtub and fill plastic flats, patting the moist soil down. My hands have learned this magic. They can sense too much water or too little, and they know how much pressure creates just enough compaction but not so much as to suffocate a sprout. Under the sunlight, beneath the greenhouse's plastic skin, the compost grows warm and humid. I adjust the great cross ventilation fans so that the temperature stays consistent through the rising daylight. Although no one sees me, the plants will bear witness, they'll testify later in volumes of green. This is how I create an even start for each seed. From the soil up.

CHAPTER TWENTY

❦

I called my mother and told her that I was leaving school to become a farmer.

I could feel her body tensing through the cell phone. I don't remember our words, just her disappointment. I tried to make excuses and promises. I thought her silence was anger over my quitting school, and that I had let her down. She didn't see farming as I did. After all, she'd escaped being a farm girl. Mom grew up in a little town where one school housed every grade. The town is tucked in the folds of the Green Mountains, high above the Connecticut Valley in a landscape called the Northeast Kingdom, or just The Kingdom if you are a local. I assumed as a girl that its name referred to heaven, but it was the last place she wanted to live. Most of her classmates stayed there, married young, and took over farms that had been in their families for generations. They managed big dairy lots with corn and hay fields, messy barns and scattered outbuildings, drafty rooms cluttered with broken toys, and stacks of bills.

In high school she escaped to Burlington, on the shores of Lake Champlain, playing in the state's youth orchestra. She kept her concert dress in the car so it wouldn't smell like a farmyard. My mother imagined farming as a death sentence. She'd seen it break bodies, and understood how limbs could be eaten by combines and bailers, or backs hunched while skin cancer spread like the pink off-road diesel over farmer's faces and arms.

"I just don't understand," she said.

"You wouldn't," I replied.

"We just want you to be happy," she said.

"I am happy," I said, but I meant *I will be happy*.

What does happiness even look like, I wondered? Happiness, I thought, is sunlight, dirty hands, worked muscle fiber pulling tight to the bone, sweat on my upper lip, heavy fruit to carry, sweetness, berries, tomato juice dripping, watching sun rise over the same land, knowing the time by the shadows' lengths, the land calling, needing, wanting me. A farm girl. With animals it's called *husbandry*, but there is no word for the female vegetable grower, married to the land.

I gave my notice of withdrawal to the school. The form required that I take it one by one to my professors to collect their signatures. I told my professors that I wouldn't be back in the fall. Some of them asked why, others didn't. If they questioned me, I told them that I needed to be closer to home or that I missed my family. What I didn't say was that my real family was a crew of farm hands working forty rolling, organic acres in Vermont. I didn't think they'd understand like my French

History teacher had. My professors were sad to see me go. They asked why had I written so well and made such good grades just to leave? I shrugged. In some ways I felt like I was giving up—and in a sense I was. I'd decided to abandon that path and move on.

When my withdrawal notice was filled with signatures, I slipped it over the desk to the admissions department officer and officially disappeared from the fall semester. Goodbye to textbooks and exams. Goodbye to academic libraries and lecture halls, to leather laptop cases, pearls and slacks. Goodbye to blow drying my hair and mornings spent doing makeup in front of the mirror.

I started to pack early, boxing up the pots and pans, sorting the books into piles on the carpet. One afternoon the moving company Jayden's mom had hired showed up and two men took away the big bed, his books, a few paintings, and a coffee table. I spread out sheets and slept on the carpet. The walls sounded empty that night. Every noise bounced back to me and the space felt suddenly huge. Wrapped up in a nest of blankets on the floor I seemed tiny and exposed, like the inside of a seed.

Two years of light had faded the paint around the pictures on the wall leaving behind pale rectangles. When the sun rose, the natural light drew out these negatives. I walked from empty wall to empty wall, admiring the lonely paint where once there were concert posters, photographs, and canvases. Had the walls darkened or was it dust? I drew my finger along the drywall. Maybe a little bit of both. Age worked in both ways—by addition and subtraction—I thought. What photos remained I took down and wrapped. Now the mantel was empty of my letterpress molds. The black and white photos of the farm which had spoken to me through the winter were hidden behind bubble wrap and stacked neatly against each other on the floor. Behind the pictures on the mantel, I found an old lighter and a fortune from Chinese takeout. It was only a smiley face icon, grinning in the center of the paper. I slipped it into the back of a picture frame for good luck.

As the apartment emptied, I began to love it more. I looked out the windows now that all the pictures were off the wall. I stood on the porch and watched sunrise and sunset over the black wall of the Cascades, ragged as sharks' teeth. Below the city was soft with green. From my perch, I was an outsider, high above the roofs of the neighborhood.

Another day, later that week, a trash company arrived and threw everything I didn't want off the balcony into a container truck they had parked below. The heavy TV, the cinderblocks that had once supported Jayden's desk, boxes and boxes of papers, and the bar stools went crashing down until the place was stripped. Everything broke apart when it landed. The violence of its departure clawed at me. But endings were never easy. With the furniture gone, the paintings just lightboxes on the walls, and my bed a nest on the floor, I felt fresh and mournful.

While packing up for the drive to Vermont I touched all my things as I set them away. I handled each book and sorted them into two piles, one for keeping and the other for selling. I smelled their pages and remembered their stories, bringing up the pine air in Michigan, salt in Maine, mud in Vermont, dry oak and rock on the coast of California, the musk of Portland's rains. Some of them I had bought with Jayden, some were schoolbooks, highlighted and dog-eared. We'd been book hunters in the desert, in the mountains, along the coasts. In the year after I graduated from high school, we'd spent a summer week in Maine at a rented cabin on some rocky bay. Each morning we fished in the secondhand books stores and antique shops in town for old hardcovers and every afternoon we sat out on the huge flat rocks at the water's edge, flipping through that day's catch. I remembered the way those moldy volumes smelled in salt, air, and sun. There was a bookstore in the desert of New Mexico in the parlor of a Victorian house just off the main street where we'd discovered my beloved edition of *Leaves of Grass*, bound in green burlap. From the high windows of that place, we'd watched a thunderstorm gallop over the mountains of Taos and across the plain to town. We'd stayed put in the bookstore until the rain passed and the high desert was bright again when we stepped out with our bags of books.

There were gifted volumes—Christmas, birthday, anniversary books, signed by our favorite authors and bought often at too high a cost, yet we'd felt it essential to have their handwriting close to our hearts. Under our fingertips, the organic swirls of signatures came to life and sprung from the page and seemed like familiar friends, not our revered masters. I'd sent some of these home with the movers to Jayden in California. The gifts I'd given him seemed too essential to sell, even if they were worth hundreds of dollars. I wasn't in the mood for more destruction. First, we'd broken, then lived through the long drag of addiction, the anxiety, the terror at his face so white on the carpet, his lips dried, then the emptying of the apartment, the breaking of furniture . . . it was all too much. I wanted to part with the books tenderly.

At the edge of the shelf, I found a hardcover collection of Emily Dickinson's poems. My grandmother had given me the book the Christmas before she died. I was just starting to read poetry then. I kept a journal with my own stammering attempts: sonnets to my dog, ballads about how much I hated school, trying to match my life to the romance of Yeats or Shakespeare. Her inscription on the first page looped around in old-fashioned cursive, like my mother's. I realized it was the only writing of hers I had, as rare as the signature of my favorite poets.

At her burial service in the family plot across from a red dairy barn I had opened the book and read a poem from it, standing very tall and adult among the gravestones. I remembered trying to keep my voice steady, like I did when I presented in class, and making sure to speak loudly over the wind and the mooing of Jersey cows. They had come up to the fence to watch the event, dipping their heads under the bottom rail to eat graveyard grass.

I flipped through the book trying to recall which of the poems I had read at the service. None of them looked familiar, but I remembered being hot in my black skirt and the smell of the barnyard and the cows. I remembered walking afterward through the graves and reading their names. A cat sat on a headstone cleaning his paws delicately. I hadn't been able to stand being with my family, in a tight, tearful cluster as the farm stayed busy and bright behind us.

I shut the book and put it in my pile of keepers.

In the morning I took the stack of books to Powell's Books and sold them for gas money. It was my last visit to that store where I'd spent so much of my time in the city. I walked in under the weight of volumes, head heavy, sweat beading along my forehead. One by one the books were inspected, scanned, and valued. The bookseller made several stacks on his table before offering me the price. Instead of taking store credit, as I always did in the past, I asked for cash. I wasn't going to be back. Returning to my car I was light, holding only a folded check in my pocket. I wasn't bound by anything but I wasn't rich either.

I imagined accumulating books as the truest form of wealth and dreamt of vast libraries with rolling ladders, shelves rising up to high ceilings, volumes filled with my notes and annotations. Selling half my collection reduced me. I worried that I'd given too much away. All my years with Jayden were now just a bank of memories and a few objects: a record player that the movers forgot and that I decided to keep, and some pictures of us, on dusty roads in the West, in which we both look happier than I remembered being. I stacked those up and slipped them into a box in my desk. Nothing grows from emptiness. All life starts from some essential ingredient. I could fit all of my belongings into a car. Books, clothing, pots and pans, pictures, even a cat. But was I too light? Had I given too much away to return to the farm?

That night I wept and my sobbing echoed off the empty walls.

Seeding becomes a ceremony. In its steady pace, I find it easy to forget time and wake, four hours later, with the sun on the other side of the greenhouses and new voices on the radio, discovering a few tables of freshly seeded flats. *Fill, seed, cover, carry, water* forms a rhythm until I complete the list for the week.

Seeding is solitary work. Outside the greenhouse, the crew circles in Yoda on their way to plant tomatoes, or they drive tractors in and out of the shop. Working in the greenhouse feels like hiding. I've always been a good hider, happy to be forgotten during a game of hide and seek. No one calls to me. I work steadily, bringing all my intent to the task as if that joy could influence the seed's growth. I become an expert in placing seeds on the soil and pressing them only just so deep.

I learn the perfect mixture of soil and water to make seeds break and sprout and where particular crops do best on the tables, and which need to be tended often and which seem to grow better when they are ignored. I think of it as an honor to be tasked with each beginning, to brush the leaf tops of thousands of starts and touch, directly, a condensed vision of the farm. Before plants grow big, they begin small and I tend then, I cup them, and water them into life.

CHAPTER TWENTY-ONE

I left Portland the morning after I took my final exam.

The night before, I packed the car carefully, the books first and then bags of clothing and bedding. I ate takeout off of paper plates, just as Jayden and I had when we first moved in. The kitchen was scrubbed clean, all my cups and plates nestled in boxes. I slept nervously, watching headlights fill the hollow space. Lights rolled over the clean walls and blank floors. My cat walked around with nothing to perch on, as restless as I was. In bed, I thought about the farm and what I missed the most. What was the first thing I'd do there, I wondered? What would I touch, smell, or see? Would my hands remember the swing of a hoe or the slice of a knife instantly, or would it take me a few days to recall those mechanics?

If I hadn't been so driven forward, I might have paused longer at that point and felt the significance of the move, the loaded car, the empty rooms, but instead all I could dream of was escaping home. Leaving was a final chapter in a love story that I thought would be my life. Although it had taken so many months to break from Jayden it still felt to me as if I was running away from him, from us. After all, I was abandoning the girl I had been for him. I didn't know if I'd ever wear makeup, or pearl earrings, or travel as I had with him. I knew my eyes would be too tired from squinting into the sun all day to read poetry at night. I knew that my mind would be hammered flat by sweat and that my journals would run dry. But I didn't know that those things would haunt me, as Jayden did in the empty apartment.

Like the oil on the handle of my hoe, which was my sweat and the sweat of many others, my story was a collection, built by accumulation. Even as I tried to ignore the past, I felt it pressing against my back. In the emptiness of the apartment, our histories lingered, walking from door to window, pacing the floor, loving and reading, fighting and drinking, writing, sleeping, sipping tea in the light of mornings past. Here we fed the cat when she first came slinking up the stairs to us, coaxing her out from under the bed with a can of tuna. Here we cooked Thanksgiving and toasted the harvest. Here we spread textbooks and fell asleep with our cheeks on the slick pages. Here we wept. Here we made love so many times that each individual act blended into a singular motion. Here we broke. Here a wine stain was scrubbed from the carpet. Here pills were crushed into powder under a heel. Here death was closer than life. Here, life began again.

At dawn I watched sunrise break over the great range of the Cascades. I'd been up before the light, anxiously checking my alarm. The hours and miles spread out ahead of me and all the while the farm beat like a drum at the end of the road, so loud it kept me up at night. Perhaps feeling the need to slow down, I made myself stop and watch the sun's first shimmer on the icy peaks. Then that star appeared, like a huge liquid drop behind the volcano's form, rising and shrinking, turning the mountains into a solid shadow and filling the valley with light. Those mountains had once marked one of the many boundaries between myself and the farm. They'd stood like a wall, fencing me into this place where I didn't belong.

Today, I told myself, I'd cross those mountains and drive into the rising sun.

I rolled up my nest of a bed into black plastic bags. Then I brushed my teeth and stuffed my backpack with toiletries. I didn't pause long enough to catch a glimpse of myself in the mirror but if I had I would have been a blur—something moving too quickly—not the thin ghost I'd been in the winter but something just as fleeting. I pushed my bags into the back of the car and nestled the cat on a soft pile of towels on the back seat. She climbed up to the top of my boxes, pressed against the roof of the car and glared at me, twitching her tail like a metronome, faster and faster.

Summer air was rising from the spruce woods. Only a few windows in the city were bright. Everyone else was still asleep. My heartbeat rose with excitement. It felt like a holiday morning. It felt like taking off. In so many dreams I'd tried to fly by running as fast as I could. In the dreams, I'd gain a little bit of air, just enough to make me believe that flight was possible, before falling back to earth. That morning I knew I'd make it. I'd begin my great migration home.

"I'm just going to check that we've got everything," I said to the cat. She eyed me anxiously as I walked up the three flights of wooden steps alone. I scanned each space. I opened the bathroom door and peeked into the shower stall. I stood in the empty kitchen where I had cooked Thanksgiving for the first time. In the living room the mantel lay naked, the walls simply white, the carpet open where I had found Jayden's body one evening. It was just a box again. I shut the door and dropped the key in the rental office.

With the sun straight ahead of me, I drove out of the city. At first, I was silent. My heart was roaring, my blood racing through my body—everything alive and pointed toward home. I felt like the tip of an arrow, or the first goose in a great flying V, pushing through the air. The city rolled into suburbs and then trees spread dark and thick into the hills.

My cat settled into her spot at the top of the car, looking out at the road through the windshield. I passed over one bridge, then another, rising, rising, up toward the mountains. Then a sense of freedom struck me as I realized that I was finally doing it: I was starting my journey east. I smiled and rolled the window down and waved my hand through the air like a swimming fish. I turned on the CD player. I took pictures with my phone of my hands on the wheel, of the rocky shoulders of the Cascades, of the huge, blue sky where it seemed the road ended.

I passed over the first mountain range and into Idaho before nightfall, stopping in a town called Snow where spring hadn't reached its warm fingers yet. I carried the cat into the hotel room with me and she stalked the strange new space while I quickly showered, ate a sandwich from a gas station and fell into bed. In the morning, well before dawn, we packed up again, stopping only to refuel the car and my stomach. Day broke over the high country, bare as bones. The road straightened and became a long line disappearing into a point on the horizon. I drove through the last shirttails of winter as I headed east. Beyond the cold roar of the wind the plains lay open and brown. Deep snowbanks still lined the higher passes.

In South Dakota, I got a flat tire in the Badlands and had to unpack the car onto the side of the road. Snow blew from the north and covered the spines of my books, the slim cases of records. The cat hid under the front seat. I turned my face away from the wind as I jacked up the car and put on the spare, afraid that I would be set back, that I would miss something at the farm. I was terrified of losing time. The wind knocked my lungs flat and I gasped to catch my breath. I drove the spare into a small-town shop where I waited for a new tire to be mounted, the cat growling from inside the elevated car whenever the mechanics passed the window. In the waiting room, I gulped down bitter coffee from a paper cup, tapping my nails on the metal armrest of my chair and wishing the work done. *Faster,* I thought, *faster. I've got to get going.* I didn't want to miss a thing; not a planting, a sunrise, a morning's harvest. I'd been waiting so long but now that

I was moving, I wanted to be back at the farm more than ever. It itched at me. It burned.

Once I was driving again, I calmed. I raced into the softness of Nebraska listening to Bob Dylan wail on his harmonica. The sunset glowed in the rearview mirror and darkness rose over the country before me, eastward. On the great interstates, I had only to navigate directionally. Each day I covered 800 miles or more.

This is not a vacation, I told myself when my eyelids drooped and I wanted to stop early, enjoy a long meal in some diner, find a bed and crash. I'd push myself to go a little farther, add a few more miles to the map before resting. I'd open the window and let the arctic air blast me awake. I knew if I had stopped or slowed down, I would have felt guilty. I didn't want to be looking at museum displays when I could be slipping starts out of their cells or cupping big pumpkin seeds in the greenhouse. A burger at a roadside restaurant would waste thirty minutes of drive time, over forty miles. I grew more anxious as I left the plains and crossed Missouri and spring bloomed green on the landscape. The plants changed and became familiar to me. Grasses flushed along the roadside and dandelions winked yellow from rolling farm fields. I was so close. The cat slept in the sun on the dashboard, lazy with heat. She'd become used to our life on the road and I talked to her as we slipped into New England, telling her of the yard where she'd hunt, of the porch where she could lay during the day while I was at work.

I drove into the night and woke early to the buzz of the alarm clock by the bedside. I stopped only for gas and

food. States fell away behind me until, at dusk, I bridged
the border of New York and Vermont and saw the gentle
rise of the Green Mountains and my heart lifted. The
mountains opened and welcomed me home. I slowed as I
passed through them, down the steep grades into the central valley. Lights from the towns along the river spread
up the dark hills, flickering like small candles. When I
rolled down my window the air was wet and smelled like
rich soil. The fields were being plowed up for the spring,
gardens planted. Everywhere there was the smell of
growing things. I silenced my radio and listened to the
rush of water from the hills, the sound of the wind in
new leaves.

There was great comfort in finding everything exactly
as I left it as I pulled into town. The pillars of Dartmouth's
library were lit like an ancient temple. Flags decorated
the lampposts on Main Street and the Green stretched
wide between the last few elm trees. Finally, my headlights swept down my family's driveway, across the apple
trees I had planted as a kid and my car stopped, settling,
in front of the garage. Outside, there was the sound of
frogs in the forest and wind in the pines. Everyone was
sleeping. I let myself in with the secret key under the step
and tiptoed upstairs with the cat. That first night I slept in
my childhood bedroom, with the cat wandering around
the new space, coming to rest, finally, beside my head.

I slept late, exhausted from the drive, and woke to the
sounds of my family taking showers and unloading the
dishwasher. The morning sun lay hot on my face when I
finally got out of bed. I changed out of my driving clothes

and stepped downstairs, one stair at a time, marveling at how similar the world was, how unchanged, while I felt so very different. Reborn. Downstairs my mother kissed me and my father hugged me in his cook's apron. I settled into a chair around the kitchen table. For the first time in days, I sat still while the world washed around me. The morning light fell pure and bright onto the tablecloth. My parents asked me about the drive and I described it in short, clipped phrases. It had been more an expedition than a trip. What had I seen but the vast land, the similar faces of rest stops, gas stations, and broken-down motels? All the time the farm had risen in my vision like a mountain through the windshield.

My father methodically measured and set the temperature on the griddle, flipped bacon, and stirred scrambled eggs. I carried orange juice and two pitchers of steaming maple syrup to the table. The syrup came to us in big plastic jugs from my mother's cousin in The Kingdom once a year. My hands were still shaking from exhaustion as I reached for the pitcher. I drowned my pancakes in syrup. It was a New Hampshire luxury, Grade A amber sweetness, the first sap of the year from the oldest trees, boiled over wood fires and bottled hot. I dipped my bacon in it and let the steam from my tea fill the pores on my cheeks. I felt soaked in the light and the smell of home. I settled down into the back of my chair.

I'd made it. I was home.

I planned to start work at the farm on Monday, so I spent the weekend unpacking the car into the apartment next to my parents' garage where they'd welcomed me to stay for as long as I wanted. This arrangement of privacy and shared space seemed ideal. I had doors I could lock and doors I could open if I felt the need for family. My grandmother used to live in the apartment and it still seemed like hers, even though they had rented it to several tenants since her death. I decided to paint the living room a bright, salmon pink, lighter than the Portland kitchen, making it my space with color. I thought my grandmother would have liked it. It was the color of the sugar-free gum she'd chew while watching TV in her armchair. This was our place. My place. I set my books up in a built-in case and it was only then that I remembered Jayden and thought of him recovering somewhere near the cold, violent beaches of California. I sat with my books just long enough to imagine his hands on their pages before slipping them into order and moving on to unpacking the kitchen.

The cat hunted in the yard and lay in the sun on the porch, exactly as I'd promised her while we raced along the interstate. I took out my farm clothing—my worn shirts and work bikini, T-shirt and tank tops, sandals, mud boots, work boots, folding knife, cord belt, baseball hat, raincoat, fleece—and organized them in the top drawers of my dresser and the front of my closest so they would be the easiest to reach. I filled my bike tires with air, cleaned out my backpack from the road trip, and stuffed it with sunscreen, Band-Aids, and water bottles.

I looked at myself in the bathroom mirror and saw someone real. I felt the strength in my arms and shoulders, pride in wrinkles near my eyes. I was ready.

⚘

I'm fifteen years old the first day I go to work at the farm. I wake up before my alarm clock, with the light just a few shades past dark. My parents have gotten up early to make me pancakes, celebrating my first day with a real job instead of the sporadic babysitting that had kept me busy during the school year. They watch me eagerly as I sponge up maple syrup with a pancake and chase that sweetness with black tea.

My mother stands in the garage with her arms crossed over her cotton nightgown, watching me approvingly as I apply sunscreen and spray myself with bug spray. She hands me my water bottle, already sweating from the heat, and a salami sandwich I packed the night before. Waving goodbye, I zip up my backpack, strap on my helmet, kick my bike off its stand and pedal up the driveway. A heavy fog blankets the river valley, devouring all sound. It is as still as the night when I ride to the farm. In the silence of dawn, I can hear myself breathing hard uphill and then the sweet click of gears as I race down. The ride is an easy thirty minutes on quiet roads. I don't see any cars, just an orange cat hunting in a patch of daylilies.

I cross a big iron bridge into Vermont, clatter over the railroad tracks, and speed down the farm road. I lay my bike against the split rail fence by the yellow farmhouse where a few days ago I'd interviewed with Kate for the job of a picker. I walk down to the strawberry shack just like she'd instructed me to do, although it is only a hunched shape in the dark. My footprints track behind me in the dew. I have gotten there early and sit on the side of the dirt road waiting for the other kids to arrive. It is so quiet at the farm that I feel like an intruder. I hold my breath a little. Tall weeds mask the rows so that all the land looks the same. The grasses and broad leaves bow under the weight of the heavy dew.

That damp silence is broken by a red pickup truck rattling down the road. An older man gets out and opens the strawberry shack without acknowledging me. I hope he is Bill, who Kate had told me I would meet by the shack, but I am too nervous to ask. I stand up and wait. The man who may be Bill keeps busy until all the kids are assembled, and then he gathers us into a rough circle. Most of the others look my age, although I don't recognize their faces. We go around and introduce ourselves, ending with the man who claps his chapped hands together and says, "I'm Bill. Now let's get down to business." He takes a quart of berries from the shack and sets it on the ground in front of his boots.

Bill has a belly like a pregnant lady but is skinny everywhere else. He wears a stained white tank top and blue Dickies. He has given this speech so many times that I can tell he isn't paying attention. His eyes, in the shade of his baseball cap, are distant and glassy.

"This," Bill says, "is a ripe strawberry." He rotates it around so that we can see that it is red on every side. He picks up another strawberry. "This one's too ripe. No good." It is deep red like wine and I can tell just by looking at it that it's squishy. Bill tosses it in the grass. "Don't pick those," he says. "You can eat them, but they don't taste too good."

He rummages around in his quart of berries until he finds one that is unripe. He holds it out in his palm. The tip is white. He flips it over and the whole backside flashes light pink. "If I see any of these in your quarts," he says, "I'll be pissed. 'Cause this berry would be perfect in a few days and now it's just trash." He pitches the underripe berry on the ground. "Nobody wants to eat that." His eyes come into focus and he looks at each of us. "If I find underripe berries in your quarts we'll have to talk. I've fired kids before for picking them."

I shudder.

Bill gives each of us a stack of ten balsa wood quarts. He shows us the clipboard where we are instructed to record the number of quarts we pick, reminding us that he'll tally all of our numbers against his final count for the day.

"No cheating," he says.

Only good quarts will earn us 75 cents. The berries have to be stacked like little volcanoes, the top berries flipped so only their ripe tips show.

Bill threatens to dump out some of the quarts that he collects and check for unripe or rotten berries. I am terrified of a bad one being discovered in mine so I only pick the best fruit, leaving behind imperfect berries for the next day. I keep my head low and work fast.

Every time I set a completed quart behind me, I make the sound of a mechanical cash register in my head, *ka-ching*, counting up my cents into dollars. I am saving for a car and for college, two expenses that seem impossible to count in berry quarts so while I rack up dollars, I am thinking mostly of being the fastest. I pick so quickly that I am suddenly ahead of the other kids in my assigned row, deep in the field and all alone.

Then a remarkable thing happens. The world unfolds. I am at peace. This shift happens so suddenly that I almost cry. My eyes are wet and I find my breathing high in my throat. My heart beats as if I'm standing next to a boy I like. I fall in love.

This feeling stays with me long after that first day picking strawberries. It happens every time I am alone at the farm in the early morning, even when I am stressed, busy, hungover, exhausted, or broken-hearted. I stop. If no one is watching, I stand up. I get out of the truck and pause. It feels like just beyond the fog, something magical is about to appear. I imagine an angel with soft grey wings like a mourning dove, or a goddess wrapped in woven corn leaves. I can almost see them shimmering at the edges of the field, about to break through into this world. They might hand me letters cut in fieldstone, or they may touch my arm and pass along a deeper truth.

That first morning as a picker I kneel low in the berry fields. My legs are wet from the straw. My fingers stain red from berries and go soft like I've been in a bath too long. The sounds of the other pickers are far behind me and there is just my breath and the rustling of the plants as I fan them out looking for fruit in their dense centers. Then the snap of the stem breaking and the shuffle of my stack of quart baskets on the straw in front of me. When

I complete a quart I set it behind me, rotating at the waist and looking back down the row at my line of quarts, the other pickers, the red farm truck at the edge of the field, the shack hunched dark near the road, and the farm beyond, painted fuzzy in soft weed-form and fog.

As the sun rises it heats the berries. It burns my back and dries out the straw rows so that they are no longer soft and damp but scratchy and scorching. My knees ache from crawling on them. Sweat drips down my forehead and falls off the tip of my nose. It stings my eyes and fills the corners of my lips with saltiness.

When the fog burns off, picking changes. It isn't soft and magical. It's tough. It's about sticking to it, fighting through the rest of the quart order, staying focused, as the heat sways my brain in waves. I stick to repetition. I let go of the pain in my knees and the heat on my back. I don't think about sweat or thirst. I become mechanical. My hands are robotic hands that shuffle in the plants. My machine knees inch forward and I bend again to the plant—shuffling, snapping, and stacking. Everything else fades away. I have no thoughts when I work in the heat. I'm not anything but the work, nothing but the quarts filled behind me like Hansel and Gretel's breadcrumb trail. I can simply count up those quarts and know where I stand. I am the girl who picks the most, every day–big, perfect quarts of berries like jewels set elegantly in balsa wood bezels.

When the sun sits at the top of the sky, right on my shoulder blades, Bill calls us into the shack. It's noon. The order is completed. Another farm hand comes in a white van and loads up the flats of berries to take to the farm stand and the grocery store in town. The pickers stand in a line, waiting to enter their numbers on the clipboard. Some of the kids go down to the dock to swim. All morning they have picked near each other and have quickly become friends but I worked alone and leave alone.

I walk back up to the barn and sit on the grassy hill that spreads down from its foundation to the fields. I eat my lunch by myself, looking over the farm. I drink all my water from the bottle and wipe my red-stained hands on the grass before pedaling home.

That first summer I work six mornings a week. At night I dream of strawberries. I look through dream-plants for them, I shuffle the leaves back, I crawl forward in straw rows, and I stack fruit up in perfect peaks. When I close my eyes, I see red berries. My knees bruise then harden. My back burns then turns a deep tan. My hands draw in soil and berry until the stains are too deep to scrub off. I sleep deeper than I imagined I could, a place so heavy that it feels like there are thick quilts over my body. I am so tired I fall asleep early and wake before the sun rises as if someone is calling me out to the field.

One day in the first week of July, Bill takes the pickers aside at noon. We have searched all morning through the dry fields looking for fruit. Our quarts are packed with tiny berries and each one takes twice as long to pick. Heat rises quicker and the day gets hot early. Insects have begun to buzz in the grass at the edge of the fields. All the yellow has left the tree leaves and the sky is hot, washed-out blue.

It's the end of strawberry season. "That's it," he says. "Today was our last harvest. Give us a call next year."

No, not yet! I think. I knew the end was coming but I don't want to believe it, I don't want to leave. The other kids race back to their bikes or rush up to the parking lot to be picked up by parents. As I walk up the dirt road I look back at the fields, at the leaves of the strawberries already speckled with red flecks of age, the straw dry and dark, no longer golden. I want to lock the image into my head: hedgerow, shack, fields, the road cutting a light, silty path between them and down to the river.

I love it here, I tell myself. I love myself here, which may be the same thing or something entirely different. I straddle my bike and ride home slowly, homesick for a memory that is still being formed.

CHAPTER TWENTY-TWO

I woke before dawn and cooked myself scrambled eggs and toast. I brewed tea and sipped it as the light rose softly over the field in my parent's backyard. Then I kicked onto my bike and pedaled up the road in a silence heavy with joy. The valley unfolded along the river, green and grey, still gently held by spring's fragility. There were no cars that morning, just the whir of bike wheels and the click of gears up the rolling hills. Dawn along the river made me want to get up early every day and not miss a single soft, beautiful transition. It was precious, this secret, soft wonder. My heart beat faster. Ahead the green metal bridge rose over the river and led me across the state line into Vermont. Cedar Circle's road sign appeared out of the fog, bright yellow and green, swinging between two posts.

I lay my bike in the cool shade of the shed, where the dirt smelled like rats and fertilizers. I'd arrived early so I could walk around a bit before the day started. I wanted to say hello to the greenhouses full of flowers, to the farm stand, and to the barn, as I had during my silent walk in December. The fields were already nearly full, each newly planted row a neat line of transplants. The river lay cool between its banks, casting swirls of mist. Above the crooked roof of the barn, a clear day bloomed. Cars and battered pickups turned into the staff parking lot and Luke and Nick strode across the road with coffee cups steaming in their hands. We quickly hugged and shook hands. *Welcome back.* Their faces were tanned and their hands still dirty. As simple as that, I was on the crew again.

One by one the field crew assembled in the processing area, where the big stainless steel sinks gleamed in the rising sun. They hiked up the hill to the barn and gathered around Yoda. Luke slipped a mix CD into the boom box above the packing table and M.I.A.'s "Paper Planes" blasted over the quiet Vermont fields. He turned the volume all the way up so that the wire racks in the processing area quivered and the sound bounced off a wall of white pines across the river in New Hampshire. Facing the growing fields and the fleet of farm trucks, with his sun-bleached T-shirt hanging loosely over his board shorts, his feet slipped into flip-flops, a switchblade knife clipped to his waistband, Luke lip-synced to the track, *no one on the corner has swagger like us / hit me on my burner prepaid wireless / we pack and deliver like UPS trucks / already going to hell just pumping that gas.*

I crossed my arms and leaned against the rough bark of the old maple tree that grew near the processing area. I shook hands with new members. I high-fived old friends. There was Robert in a floppy sun hat with a punk rock tattoo of a screaming skull on his left arm, and James in short 70s running shorts, Nicolas and Eileen looking like they'd just hopped off a train, Charlie looking dazed and confused with messy blond curls, and Hazel in an American flag bikini and huge dangling earrings.

Nick opened a box of gas-station donuts on the hood of the farm truck and we each reached into the box and grabbed one. Half of us smoked cigarettes under the maple tree, chasing the nicotine with a sticky bite of donut. Itchi slipped by, walking along the split rail fence by The Yellow House on his way to hunt mice in the blackberries.

Luke planned the day on a whiteboard hung in the processing area and every morning the crew drew around it like moths, anxious to see what we would be doing that day. This was our morning ritual. Luke stood off to the side, smoking, finishing his donut and watching us react to his plans. He laughed at any complaints and told us he loved us. That morning Luke put most of the crew out planting a long row of lettuce, but not me. I had been at the farm long enough to develop a set of specialized skills, picked up summer by summer, which placed me slightly higher up the ladder. Seniority was very important in the field crew. It meant knowing who you had to respect and who you could tell to fuck off. It meant the difference between bitch work and the honor of a title like seeder or tractor driver or crew leader. My first job that morning, according to Luke's notes on the whiteboard, was to pick asparagus. He had scribbled my name next to a long dash followed by his shorthand, *asparagus.*

Nick and Luke gathered the rest of the crew into the bed of one of the pickup trucks.

Luke grabbed a dirty three-ring binder where his master plan for the fields was stored. Sitting in the driver's seat, he flipped through the printed pages until he found the field number and row for the morning's lettuce. In a swift motion, he slammed the binder shut, flung it onto the dashboard, flipped the CD player onto the one CD that still played in that truck: *Blood Sugar Sex Magik* by the Red Hot Chili Peppers, and shifted into gear. The crew in the bed jolted and then settled as they drove off to the greenhouse to load up transplants.

I grabbed a harvesting tote and a sharp serrated knife from the barn and tossed them in the back of the remaining vehicle, an old red Toyota truck. My feet and hands remembered its clutch. This was the original farm truck. A host of trucks would come and die on the farm—last-leg work vehicles, rusted thin, with clutches like ghosts and gears as sticky as old latches. Every one of them had a name, mostly out of convenience. There was Strider, Obi-Wan, Vader, Wanda, Ben, and The Tundra. But from the first summer Will and Kate took ownership of Cedar Circle to the day I left, one truck remained, working through all those seasons

Over the years it would have its tailgate replaced, its back windows knocked out, and its headlights and taillights smashed. It became increasing picky about music in its last years and would spit out anything except the *Best of Tina Turner.* The radio worked for another five seasons then it too crashed into a sizzle of static.

The brakes were butter soft. The clutch became just a mechanical memory, a trick of the foot. The parking brake light was always on although there wasn't a parking brake. Sometimes, on a drunken night, someone would discover that the headlights still worked. In the summer the vents blew warm air because the AC hadn't been recharged in a decade. But come fall the heat still pumped warm and strong, coughing up a season's worth of dirt and pollen.

We tried but often forgot to roll up the windows when it rained so in the summer Yoda's seats were damp from storms, irrigation or the wet backsides of swimmers. We slept in the bed under the stars by the river. We pulled that truck out of mud and snow, skated it over ice, and drove its small engine to heartbreak dragging trailers loaded with squash and pumpkins. Yoda was always dirty, inside and out, and developed a unique smell of mold, soil, human, oil and gas, rusted metal parts and soft vegetables. It was a gentle, hardworking truck. I once told Nick I wanted to write a poem about Yoda and he said it will have to be as long as the Odyssey.

Over twenty teenagers learned how to drive a stick shift in its cab, lurching on the safe farm roads until they learned the right combination of gas and clutch and slipped the gears into rolling. Nick and Luke had taught me to drive it when I was seventeen, sweating behind the wheel as they hollered from the bed, *let it out, let it out, give it gas, gentle, slow down!*

I learned that to get into four-wheel drive you shifted into neutral but to get out of it you had to speed up and change back into two-wheel drive while in second gear. H4 was for muddy roads but never pavement. L4 was for heavy loads and low speed. My feet worked the pedals like a pianist. The smooth black plastic head of the gear-shift was a lucky charm in my right palm. The seat belts didn't latch but we never wore them. We laughed at the new crew members that tried to put them on.

No. This is a farm truck, we'd say.

That first morning back I threw Yoda into second, and then raced into third on the paved road. The asparagus patch grew near the blueberries, in an overgrown lot of fern and black locust. The Stones, who had been the original owners of Cedar Circle, had planted it in a summer no one remembered. The asparagus rows were now just waves of ferns in a wild field.

I carried a red knife and a mesh shopping bag to hold my harvest. In mid-summer asparagus grew into billowing soft foliage, but in late spring the plants were tender spears, breaking secretively through grass and weed. The petals on the tip were a lighter green than the shaft. The juice that ran from a cut stem tasted like fresh English peas. Because the patch had been neglected for a decade and overrun with weeds, harvesting the asparagus became more like gathering than picking a crop. Only the most experienced crew who knew how to see the good in all that wilderness were allowed to hunt it.

I stepped silently through the tall grass, focusing on spearheads, on two-toned, pea-flavored ferns. I walked up and down the field until the sun broke through the mist. Dew dried off grasses and the day settled hot between the river and the hills.

Sometimes I talked to myself while I picked, rehearsing speeches, daydreaming, or going back in time to say or do the things I should have said. But that first morning in May I was as quiet as I could be. I listened to my body's sounds—my feet, my skin-to-skin swishing, and my finger bones clutching tight on the knife. Cars passed on the road. Yoda's engine settled like an old dog dreaming. A boat motored by on the river and the wake rustled the shore. Birds sang and shuttled in the oaks and locusts. Bumblebees buzzed inside the white, bell-shaped blueberry flowers.

When I drove back, bare feet on the hot petals of Yoda, with dirty hands and sunburn flushing my shoulder blades, I was again something solid. I was a farmer.

ACKNOWLEDGMENTS

Many hands have shaped this story. I would like to thank Ann Hood and Connie May Fowler who, as my advisors at Vermont College of Fine Arts, guided the very first drafts of this project into fruition. In addition, thanks to Patrick Madden, who reminded me that the value of nonfiction is the truthiness of the thing, that I am the I, the girl who decided to move back home and farm. Thank you to Dede, Rose, and Ferne at Green Writers Press who understood the book and helped make it stronger with their passion and guidance. Thank you to Daniel and my dogs who watched over me as I wrote and rewrote this book over the course of many years. Although the book itself is testament to their strength and beauty, thank you to my friends who, so many years ago, became my farm family, my crew, and who grew with me over the seasons through all of the effort, all of the sweat, blood, and tears. Luke, Nick, Sarah, Justin. Finally, I give my deepest thanks to the land itself, to its history both geological and human, its old soil, well loved. Still those acres by the river at Cedar Circle remain sacred to me in a way that even all of these words can't explain. I am forever grateful for what the work of farming has taught me.

The crew at Cedar Circle Farm, circa 2008.